The Intext Series in
FINANCIAL MANAGEMENT

The Finance Function

The Finance Function

Leslie P. Anderson
Colorado State University

Vergil V. Miller
Sacramento State College

Donald L. Thompson
Slippery Rock State College

Intext Educational Publishers
Scranton   Toronto   London

Editor's Note

The International Textbook Series in Financial Management was designed with three purposes in mind. First, to provide textbooks for university-level courses with primary emphasis on financial decision making. Second, to provide the financial practitioner with technical information and decision-making techniques. Third, to permit maximum flexibility in course and curriculum design within the broader scope of financial management. In this regard a large selection of original works will be offered, high in intellectual quality and content. All materials offered in the series will deal with the broadening scope of the field of financial management, the theoretical foundations, the relevant intra- and interdisciplinary nature of the facets of the financial management field, the influence of modern analytical decision-oriented techniques, and the decision-making aspects of financial management problems.

The general pace of the evolution of thought in the field of financial management has recently accelerated. Significant innovations have added new complexity to the field of financial management and existing problems are being met with new approaches. As the technology advances, the traditional lines of demarcation become indistinguishable between such areas as institutional finance, financial management, investments, and money and capital markets. Since these intradisciplinary interactions affect the analysis of complex problems, they are now attracting attention from both scholars and practitioners. Hence the need for a series with appeal for both groups. Moreover, tools of analysis from economics, mathematics, statistics, computer science, and behavioral science are being applied to these problems. Topics covered in each volume place primary emphasis on these tools of analysis in an intradisciplinary setting.

Preface

Finance is a consideration in nearly all types of organized activity. While this book is addressed to the businessman, he is far from alone in his concern with problems of financial management. This book treats finance within the context of a functional system of management. The emphasis is on an integrated treatment of the three principal functions of management: finance, marketing, and production.

The purpose of this book is to help the reader better understand the major management problems faced by the business executive. This is done by setting forth these problems in a modern corporate context, and by concentrating on methods by which they may be analyzed and, hopefully, solved. The approach taken is systemic; funds sources and funds uses are considered within the same framework and in relation to each other, and in terms of the firm's internal structure and its external environment.

The book may be put to a number of uses. It may for example serve as the central text in a general (first) course in management, supplemented by other materials of the instructor's choice. These could be case materials, sections from textbook treatments of the other functional areas, or selected articles from the literature. In choosing supplemental materials, the references at the ends of the chapters should prove helpful.

Graduate and undergraduate finance majors should also find the book a useful summary of current thinking in their field. Furthermore, its clarity of treatment suits the book to this purpose and should also make the volume a welcome and ready reference for middle- and top-level business executives, regardless of their functional allegiance. It might well become recommended reading for numerous individuals seeking to gain a clearer understanding of the finance function.

To help the reader, we now offer a brief preview of the book's eight chapters, emphasizing the relationship of each of the chapters to the book's central argument. We start off with a discussion of what is meant by finance and the finance function. The first chapter summarizes the principal viewpoints taken over time, and sets forth what the authors feel is a contemporary view. In the second chapter the writers seek initially to broaden the perspective of the text—which turns from narrow consideration of finance to the very broad subject of corporate management, with finance only one of several critical factors. After defining the role of the financial manager in the first chapter, our attempt then is to relate his role to that of his functional counterparts in the areas of marketing and production.

Chapter 3 deals with the administration of the finance function. Important subissues included are the various titles given to the executive responsible for financial decisions, and where such executives are pictured in corporate organization charts. To bring these issues into better perspective, we offer case studies of four large firms.

Chapters 4 and 5 discuss investment decisions. While investments are usually looked on as a use of funds, we also seek to show how decisions made in this area also involve considerations of the *sources* of funds. Our discussion of the investment decision centers around investment alternatives—their definition, evaluation, quantification, ranking and choice. Critical in the whole process is the extent to which account is taken of time and uncertainty. The models for investment analysis around which this section is organized become successively more complex as they seek to move from the certain world of theory to that of uncertainty which is characteristic of reality.

Chapter 6 seeks to examine the other side of the coin—financing decisions. But just as we found that investment decisions could not be treated solely in terms of funds uses, we also found that financing decisions involve more than considerations of funds sources. In this area, the key issues that emerge are the cost of capital and the extent to which the firm can develop an optimal combination of funds sources.

Dividend policy is given separate consideration in Chapter 7 as an issue which involves both funds sources and funds uses. This is true to such a degree that it would have been inappropriate to include it in either the investment or the financing chapters. Our discussion of the search for an optimal dividend policy necessarily leads in the direction of serious consideration of investor behavior. Several models are introduced which treat dividend evaluation as an issue subsidiary to the broader question of valuation of the firm as a whole. The critical consideration in the analysis ultimately turns out to be the relationship between dividend policy and share values—an issue that brings the discussion very much into the real world of uncertainty.

The final chapter of the book represents an attempt to integrate the role of the financial manager, as developed, into commonly defined patterns of corporate organization. In effect, it takes the viewpoint, "If this is the way financial managers make decisions, what are the consequences for the firm as a whole?" Some attention is given to the problems of functional coordination and interaction, with the ultimate argument centering on the normative relevance of the systemic view.

While representing the collaboration of three authors, the form of this collaboration did not necessarily result in a parceling out of responsibilities for separate chapters. Instead, we share equally in the responsibility for the book's entire content. In seeking to strike out in a new direction, we received help from persons too numerous to mention. Their participation has served to make this a more significant book, and any errors are entirely our own.

Leslie P. Anderson
Vergil V. Miller
Donald L. Thompson

February, 1971

Contents

The Finance Function

Development of the Finance Function

> It must be said and said whatever men may
> think of it, that finances touch everything, help
> everything and conclude everything.
> —T. H. Russell

The finance function is often spoken of as if it were something unique and definable. However, like beauty, it may be argued that the finance function exists largely in the eye of the beholder. The finance function has been defined differently by different writers, and differently over time. Textbooks in finance are mute testimony of this.

The purpose of this chapter is to set forth the major alternative views of what has been termed the finance function and to present, in conclusion, the authors' view which emphasizes how finance is related to other activities within a firm. The view taken is general and is therefore applicable to any business, irrespective of size or legal form.

INTRODUCTION

The word *finance* came to the English language from the French and originally referred to the payment of a ransom. One of the earliest references which fixes its use in the English language is to be found in 1439 in the diary of Parl Rolls: "Whereas the seid countess hath made a lone of MCCLI to the seid Erle of Somerset for the payment of his fenaunce. . . ." Changes in the meaning of the word are documented by Hall's *Chronicle,* which in 1548 had the following to say: "In like robes following the lordes . . . of the finances. . . ." Here it is generally conceded that the reference was to the revenues of the state. By 1721 finance was looked on as the lending of money at interest. For example, Strype in Chamberlain's Letter No. 8 observes "there was no money to be had at finance in Antwerp under 16 in the hundred for one year."[1]

The word finance today generally refers to the management of money. Turning finance into an adjective and relating it to the word function results in the following definition for the finance function: *the application of skills or care in the manipulation, use, and control of money.* This is as far as the dictionary goes. There is, however, an error in relying too heavily on the dictionary. As may be seen from the above, about the only conclusion one may make with respect to the word finance is that it has a marvelous ability to evoke different concepts in the minds of men. To continue this inquiry, we must turn from dictionaries and observe what is taking place in the world about us. Let us do this by referring to some of the observations and conclusions of those who have written about the finance function.

VARIOUS VIEWS OF THE FINANCE FUNCTION

What is the proper concern of finance? Broadly categorized, three types of answers have been offered to this question:[2]

1. The first looks on finance as being concerned with cash. This is termed the *cash* approach. Since almost all business transactions ultimately have to do with cash, virtually every activity within the firm is the concern of the financial manager.

2. Another asserts that finance is concerned with raising funds. This, for reasons to be stated, is termed the *traditional* approach. This approach addresses itself almost exclusively to the procedures for raising long-term capital. The firm is visualized from the outside, in particular, from the point of view of the investment banker.[3] It should be pointed out that many students of finance and business still consider this to be the core of finance.

3. A third approach holds that finance is concerned with *both* obtaining funds and the optimal use of these funds. This is termed the *contemporary* or *problem-centered* approach. It looks on the financial man-

---

[1]See *Chamberlain's Letters,* edited by N. E. McClure (Philadelphia: American Philosophical Society, 1939). See also *The Chamberlain Letters,* edited by E. M. Thompson (New York: G. P. Putnam's Sons, 1965).

[2]For a summarized version of alternative answers to this question see Ezra Solomon, *Theory of Financial Management* (New York: Columbia University Press, 1963), pp. 2–8.

[3]At one time, and under a particular set of circumstances, this approach had real significance and probably did emphasize that aspect of the firm's finances of the greatest importance. For an excellent view, see Arthur Stone Dewing, *Financial Policy of Corporations,* 5th ed. (New York: Ronald Press, 1953).

ager as having the responsibility for raising funds in such a manner that the firm obtains capital at the lowest cost. This results in an optimal capital structure, and in so investing funds that certain goals or objectives are maximized.

The first approach in its concern with cash is too broad. Since every transaction is ultimately expressed in terms of cash, it involves the financial manager in the details of every activity. Implicitly, no allowance is made for the specification of other managerial roles within the firm.

The second approach with its emphasis on capital-raising activities is too restrictive, and today is generally rejected on this ground. This approach owes its origin to a number of causes, among which were the growth of corporations as the dominant form of business, expansion of public ownership, the merger movements, and the development and organization of the securities markets. Further, a particular author, Arthur S. Dewing, championed this approach in his classic textbook.[4] Widespread acceptance of Dewing's work led to his approach being termed the *traditional* approach to corporation finance.

The Traditional Approach

The traditional approach to finance, it may be charged, overemphasized certain things at the expense of others. What were some of these? Four problem areas may be identified.

First, students of finance tended to view the subject, and hence the firm, from the outside. The day-to-day problems of the financial manager were seldom topics for discussion. Instead, problems dealing with the underwriting of corporate offerings, agency marketing, competitive bidding, and the like, took precedence over the more immediate problems of working capital and asset management.

Another shortcoming stemmed from overemphasis on "corporation" finance and lack of treatment of noncorporate enterprises. In the American economy the corporation has become the dominant and most important form of business organization; nevertheless, a meaningful concept of financial management not only applies to corporations but should be concerned with all forms of profit-seeking enterprise.

Third, the traditional approach to financial management overemphasized certain problems that arise only infrequently during a corporation's life cycle. These include incorporation, consolidation, recapitalization, and reorganization. While such subjects are given consideration in the teaching of finance

[4]Dewing, *op. cit.*

today, there has been a shift in emphasis to the more frequent and pressing problems of the management of ongoing operations and planning for the future.

A fourth area of overemphasis was on long-term financing. Contemporary financial management also stresses the importance of short-term working-capital management and the development of analytical tools for this purpose.[5] This is not to imply that long-term financing considerations have become less important; certainly they have not. Rather, the shift in emphasis strikes a more equitable balance between short-term and long-term financing problems.

It is useful and relevant to point out these defects in the traditional approach to finance. To learn from one's mistakes and formulate plans for improving the status quo, one must be aware and cognizant of where one's shortcomings lie. So it is with finance. However, it should be recognized that most of the faults mentioned above affected the teaching of finance rather than its practical application. Problems of working-capital management, investment decisions, financial planning in the face of uncertainty, and so on have always faced the financial manager. The point is that financial management as traditionally taught did not train a person to cope with these problems. And herein lies the greatest, all-encompassing defect of the earlier viewpoint toward finance—it was too descriptive. It provided an extensive, but primarily descriptive, treatment of procedures and of financial institutions, while neglecting to equip students with the analytical tools necessary to make defensible decisions on financial problems. It is only in the past ten years or so that academicians and theorists have turned their attention to developing analytical methods designed to assist the financial manager in the decision-making process.

In conclusion, the traditional approach viewed finance as a staff specialty. The finance department would see to it that funds were available, and that was all. It would have little if anything to say about how such funds would be allocated and what the criteria for allocation should be. In short, its role, while active in the pursuit of funds, would be *passive* with respect to the distribution of those funds. For these reasons the traditional approach is now judged too narrow.

The Problem-Centered Approach

The contemporary approach to financial management is problem-centered. Since the end of World War II the case study has increasingly been used as an aid in learning how to analyze and solve typical and recurring problems of

---

[5]Solomon, *op. cit.*, pp. 5–6.

financial management. The interest in the case-study method stems from a desire for a more analytical approach. Furthermore, the trend is for such cases to be organized around, and related to, models designed to aid in the decision-making process.

With this increasing emphasis on a problem-centered approach, one is bound to ask: What problems does the financial manager typically face? Let us start with four.

1. What expenditures should the firm make?
2. What volume of funds should the firm commit?
3. How should the required funds be financed?
4. How can the firm maximize its profitability from existing and proposed commitments?

The problem-centered approach, as portrayed diagramatically in Figure 1-1, is the one advocated by the authors. Such an approach considers business in its totality, as an action system. The firm is looked on as making an inter-related series of decisions with respect to sources of funds *and* their uses.

Figure 1-1

Contemporary or Problem-Centered Approach to Finance Function

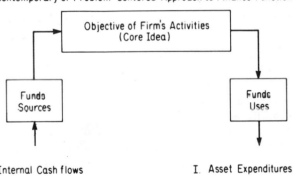

Objective of Firm's Activities
(Core Idea)

Funds Sources

Funds Uses

I. Internal Cash flows from operations and special transactions

II. External Debt or equity funds supplied by:

   A. Individuals
   B. Financial institutions or intermediaries
   C. Other business firms
   D. Government

I. Asset Expenditures

   A. Current
   B. Fixed

II. Nonasset Expenditures

   A. Labor
   B. Interest and debt service charges

III. Distributions to Owners and / or losses

Such decisions are affected by whatever objective (or objectives) the firm may seek, and the core idea around which it is organized.[6] This core idea gives the firm stability, and is expressed in terms of specific products produced or services supplied. Ultimately the core idea must meet the test of market acceptance. This forms the backdrop, the ultimate constraint, against which the financial manager's decisions are made. In making decisions as to the sources of funds, one knows that they have a cost, that they are probably not available continuously over time, and are not available in limitless amounts. Further, because of uncertainty and the legal relationship of the various security holders to the firm (priority of claims on earnings and assets), it is probable that each financing decision may affect future financing in terms of either its cost, its availability, or both. The questions, then, to be asked about the sources of funds are these:

1. From what sources are funds available?
2. To what extent are funds available from these sources?
3. What is the cost of funds presently used?
4. What is the expected cost of future financing?
5. Is there an optimal structure of liabilities as related to funds costs, and, if so, what is it?
6. Given possible constraints on funds' availability, and given that funds have a cost, what should be the structure of the firm's liabilities? Is there a conflict between that liability structure which provides funds at the lowest cost and that which provides for greatest ease and assurance of future financing? If so, how is this issue resolved?
7. Given sources of funds and their cost, what sources should be tapped, and to what extent?

To answer the above questions, the financial manager must consider the following: *How will the funds be used? What return will they earn? What risk is associated with the individual and collective uses to which they will be put?* These are, of course, questions relating to the *uses* of funds. As shown in Figure 1-1, there are three possible uses of funds: asset expenditures, non-asset expenditures, and distributions to owners. Committing funds to uses involves simultaneous consideration of sources; source decisions cannot be made independently of use considerations; and both sets of decisions must relate to the firm's objective or objectives and its core idea.

---

[6]For a discussion of the core idea concept, see Wroe Alderson and Paul E. Green, *Planning and Problem Solving in Marketing* (Homewood, Ill.: Richard D. Irwin, Inc., 1964), p. 8.

A NOTE ON THE CONCEPTS OF SYSTEM

The concepts of system—and there appear to be several—can be useful in describing what occurs in a complex organization such as a business firm, and, more importantly, in analyses to discover both reasons why a firm operates as it does, along with the chief factors causing it to operate in such a manner. The notion of system in various forms is increasingly serving as a basis for studies of many aspects of management.[7]

There is no single definition or series of definitions of system which adequately conveys the descriptive and analytical purposes to which the concept may be put. The concept seems greater than the total of its definitions. The moment a definition is propounded an example may be found which cannot be made to fit the statement. One statement representative of the better, more comprehensive definitions is:

> A system is a set of objects (parts or components) together with relationships between the objects and between their attributes.[8]

Another definition:

> . . . System . . . may be described generally as a complex of elements or components directly or indirectly related in a causal network, such that each component is related to at least some others in a more or less stable way within any particular period of time.[9]

We are of course most familiar with references to the solar system and the human body viewed as a system in whole or in part—the digestive system, the circulatory system, and the like.[10] The usage of the term applied to the solar system suggests a patterned relationship of physical bodies with an

[7]For detailed study see Richard A. Johnson, Fremont E. Kast and James E. Rosenzweig, *The Theory and Management of Systems* (New York: McGraw-Hill Book Company, 1963); Thomas B. Glans, et al., *Management Systems* (New York: Holt, Rinehart and Winston, Inc., 1968); Stanley Young, *Management: A Systems Analysis* (Glenview, Ill.: Scott, Foresman and Company, 1966); and Peter P. Schoderbek, *Management Systems* (New York: John Wiley & Sons, Inc., 1967).

[8]A. D. Hall and R. E. Fagen, "Definition of System," *General Systems*, I (1956), p. 18.

[9]Walter Buckley, *Sociology and Modern Systems Theory* (Englewood Cliffs, N.J.: Prentice-Hall, Inc., 1968), p. 40.

[10]Kenneth Boulding, "General Systems Theory: The Skeleton of Science," *Management Science*, 2 (April 1956), pp. 197–208.

ordered movement; the term when applied to the human body conveys the greater impression of life—a living, breathing organism ingesting organic material and capable of performing tasks. The former use of the term is more mechanical in outlook; the latter, more biological or organismic. The mechanical construct (which could be termed the Newtonian view) suggests a state of static equilibrium; the biologic system, a life-maintaining steady-state or homeostatic condition.

The concept of system is rooted usually within one or the other of these two views. Social scientists employing the notion, generally tending more toward the organismic disposition, have commonly elaborated their systemic views to consider the inputs into the system, and the conversion process within that system by which the inputs are rearranged in some manner and from which some output results. In this process an input unit may receive added value—such as the student who presumably enjoys an increase in knowledge and ability to perform tasks as a result of the system's interaction with him. It is also recognized that all of this takes place within an *environment,* that the system has certain *boundaries,* and that during the whole of the process *feedback* may occur at many points to cause the system to adapt its output in some way or adapt itself—even to the point of self-destruction.

As the concept has been elaborated a third view is developing especially applicable to social organizations—the "process" or adaptive perspective as suggested recently by Buckley.[11] The key to this view is *relationship* or *organization.*[12] The elements in the system then become important (insofar as the system is concerned) as they relate to and interact with one another.

> The equilibrium model, [the mechanical view] . . . is applicable to types of systems which, in moving to an equilibrium point, typically lose organization and then tend to hold that minimum level. . . . Homeostatic [organismic] models apply to systems tending to maintain a given, relatively high, level of organization against ever-present tendencies to reduce it. The process, or complex adaptive system, model applies to systems characterized by the elaboration or evaluation of organization: . . . they thrive on, in fact depend on, "disturbances" and "variety" in the environment.[13]

[11]Buckley, *op. cit.,* p. 40.

[12]This point is stressed in a useful work relating to education; R. Jean Hills, *The Concept of System* (Eugene, Ore.: University of Oregon, Center on the Advanced Study of Educational Administration, August 1967). Another education-oriented work is Martin I. Taft and Arnold Reisman, *The Education Institution as a System—A Proposed Generalized Procedure for Analysis,* ERIC, ED 012105 (1967).

[13]Buckley, *op. cit.,* p. 40.

Figure 1-2

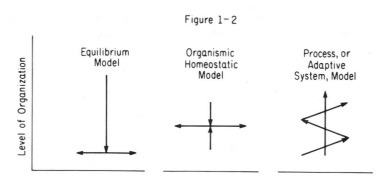

Graphically the distinctions may be shown as suggested by Buckley[14] in Figure 1-2.

The "process" or adaptive view of the system appears to suggest activity and change through time rather than static immobility. It is perhaps most relevant to conceptions of business organizations.

Using any of the above perspectives the observer may treat the system as being *open* or *closed*—or open only to certain influences. The general social system may be the subject of examination,[15] the international system,[16] a system of governments,[17] and so on from views of macro systems to those of a micro nature.

In discussing a system one may also consider in general or specific terms the *functions*[18] of that system and the structural factors responsible for the performance of those functions. Here the system view becomes linked to functionalist concerns in what is termed structural-functionalism.[19] These functional aspects have their parallel in the "objectives" or "outcomes" of the profit-and-loss-type systemic analysis of the finance or business manager.

Little has been said so far of the particular use of "system" in the performing of technical, often quantified analyses of particular problems. The use of system in this context may be placed under the rubric "systems analy-

[14]*Ibid.*

[15]Talcott Parsons has been perhaps the most influential in this regard. For a summarization of a part of his thought—by himself—see his article, " 'Voting' and the Equilibrium of the American Political System," in Eugene Burkick and Arthur J. Brodbeck (eds.), *American Voting Behavior* (New York: The Free Press, 1959), pp. 80–120.

[16]Morton A. Kaplan, *System and Process in International Politics* (New York: John Wiley & Sons, Inc., 1964).

[17]Frank P. Sherwood and Richard W. Gable, *The California System of Governments* (Belmont, Calif.: Dickenson Publishing Company, 1968).

[18]Herein considered to be "observed outcomes of patterned behavior" in the case of any social system.

[19]For amplification see for example, H. V. Wiseman, *Political Systems: Some Sociological Approaches* (New York: Praeger Publishers, Inc., 1966).

sis."[20] At the risk of gross oversimplification it may be said this is a technique of problem analysis wherein a productive "system" is analyzed in terms of the inputs required to achieve the given product or objective. The whole of the process is subject to analysis in terms of the required costs and the benefits derived. Such analyses of systems as suggested here stress the quantifiable. Systems analysis is seen as a tool for policy making in that analysis can be performed given certain alternatives and the desired outcomes. It is, moreover, integral to advanced conceptions of programming, planning, and budgeting systems (PPBS—and here note the use of the concept system).

The foregoing is not all there is to say about "system"—far from it. We have not mentioned advanced approaches in information theory, cybernetics, or decision-making model developments and their relatedness to concepts of system. We do not pretend to be sufficiently familiar with all uses of the concept. We are not familiar with enough of the writings of those who have contributed to its development to be able definitively to set forth what is or what is not subsumed under a label such as General Systems Theory; or even to state if there *is* such a body of thought of sufficient order to be considered a "theory" or related group of theories.

Our purpose here is to point up the fact that there are various meanings connoted by "system" representing differing approaches, differing levels of abstractions, and differing degrees of exactitude. But from these differing meanings and usages of the concept we may now suggest some possibly fruitful avenues of investigation about financial management using a systems posture or perspective.

FINANCE AND OTHER MANAGEMENT FUNCTIONS

The financial manager in the systemic view cannot make decisions alone or in a vacuum. Decisions affecting sources and uses of funds and attainment of corporate objectives should involve the active participation of executives in every functional area. The firm should be viewed as a system. For example, the decision to purchase a capital asset is based on expected net return from its use, and on the associated risk. These cannot be given values by the financial manager alone. Instead he must call on the expertise of those in other functional areas: marketing, production, accounting, personnel. Thus the contemporary or problem-centered approach to finance looks for help where needed and appropriate. The financial decision is looked on as cutting across

[20]This term is somewhat unfortunate in that any consideration of "system" can be an "analysis." But common usage appears to have delimited an area of "systems analysis."

functional, even disciplinary, boundaries. It is in such an environment that the financial manager works as a part of total management. Hopefully, the finance function as conceived contributes to the integration of efforts of those in all functional areas.

SUMMARY AND CONCLUSIONS

This chapter represents the first step in our investigation of the nature of the finance function. It is concerned with the manner in which teachers of finance have developed approaches which ignore or distort things financial managers actually do. An attempt is also made to advocate a systemic approach which, if adopted, hopefully will lead to the financial manager's being better able to do his job.

Held up for special criticism are those approaches to financial management that have sought or tended to make it a narrow, specialized discipline. Instead, it is argued that *financial* decisions are *business* decisions. They affect the destiny of the firm as a whole, they cannot be made independently of decisions in other functional areas, and they cannot ignore the firm's environment.

Despite its title, this book is as much concerned with decision making as with finance. The primary interest is what financial managers do and should be doing, and how they might be more analytic in approaching problems with which they are faced. The point of reference is always the firm, looked on as seeking to profitably exploit some core idea. Decisions as to sources and uses of funds are viewed as being made in terms of the core idea, but with further reference to whatever objective or objectives individuals within the firm might be seeking, or perceive themselves as seeking. Despite the difficulties encountered in so doing, the question of the firm's objectives is one that must be faced before the role of any single decision maker within the firm can be evaluated.

SUGGESTED REFERENCES

"The New Power of the Financial Executives," *Fortune*, 65 (January 1962), pp. 81–85, 138, 143.
Firmin, Peter A. and James J. Linn, "Information Systems and Managerial Accounting," *Accounting Review*, 43 (January 1968), pp. 75–82.
Hindricks, H. J., "Finance on the Frontier," *Financial Executive*, 32 (March 1964), pp. 51–54.

Meltzer, Allan H., "Discussion, Developments in the Curriculum and Teaching of Finance," *Journal of Finance*, 21 (May 1966), pp. 424–427.

Moag, Joseph S., Willard T. Carleton, and Eugene M. Lerner, "Defining the Finance Function: A Model-Systems Approach," *Journal of Finance*, 22 (December 1967), pp. 543–556.

Robbins, Sidney, and Edward Foster, Jr., "Profit Planning and the Finance Function," *Journal of Finance* 12 (December 1957), pp. 451–467.

Schiff, Jack, and Michael Schiff, "The Role of Accounting in Marketing: A Dialogue Between Professors Jack and Michael Schiff," *Sales Management*, 95 (December 3, 1965), pp. 36–38, 40, 42.

Weston, J. Fred, "The Finance Function," *Journal of Finance*, 9 (September 1954), pp. 265–282.

Finance and the Management Functions

If you don't know where you're going, any road will take you there.—Theodore Levitt

A deceptively simple way of studying business firms is to look on them as groups of individuals perceiving themselves as doing something that presumably relates to some general idea of what the end result of their activities is expected to accomplish. Implicitly this assumes that the firm's members: (a) are trying to accomplish something, and (b) are organized in some manner and with some purpose in mind.

Membership in a business firm does not come "naturally" to individuals. Business requires a person to take on a series of arbitrarily defined roles. In a free society, participation in any specific productive activity is voluntary. However, to come to the heart of the matter, many of those so engaged would probably prefer to do something else, somewhere else. Also, merely by assuming a role in a business organization, an individual does not cast aside other roles that he might fill simultaneously: head of a family, member of a political party, member of a church. That role conflict and personal considerations affect business decision making is undeniable. The discussion below does not ignore this fact, but rather examines the extent to which a person's behavior in a business organization is affected by beliefs he might have as to its objectives or purpose. Specifically, the emphasis is on the concept of a corporate objective as it affects the roles taken on by the firm's principal decision makers.

CORPORATE OBJECTIVES

Textbooks talk of the company "objective." In the development of this concept, economics and semantics have at times become hopelessly intertwined. Recent attempts at articulating this objective have replaced the concept of "profit maximization" by the more sophisticated concept of "wealth maximization." The latter regards the firm as attempting to maximize the discounted value of an expected income stream. Ignoring the level of analysis for a moment, all statements of corporate objectives ultimately return to the basic issue of how to maximize return. The desire, it seems, is to describe company behavior in this respect by a single, all-inclusive statement. Presumably such simplification facilitates study of a firm's activities by virtue of knowledge as to where they lead. But the danger is that one can forget a simplification has been made. Soon the simplification blends into pseudo-reality, and the trap is closed.

Commonly the premise is made that there are clearly defined and generally accepted company objectives, and that the company is managed in light of these objectives. However, companies are run by individuals occupying roles both corporately and personally defined. These people, with varying responsibilities and backgrounds, seek different and at times mutually exclusive or conflicting objectives. Too often it is assumed that those in management are concerned only with the attainment of objectives beneficial to the corporation. Is this meaningful? How quickly is Mr. X likely to forsake his lavish expense account or his next raise to insure that his department maximizes its long-run contribution to corporate wealth? Management personnel have objectives divergent from the ones commonly assumed by students of business. Moreover, these objectives are actively pursued. The costs generated by Mr. X's pet projects may be hidden in overhead accounts or in some other fashion made palatable to critical observers such as stockholders or higher management: observers whose objectives may differ not only from lower management but from each other.

What then may be done about this problem of defining corporate objectives? One possible solution is to *assume* that firms seek to maintain a working balance among the claims of the various groups exerting an influence on them. In effect this involves the attainment of a giant compromise. Somehow there is attained a satisfactory reconciliation of the interests of the management, which wants more profit and continuity of operations, the customer, who would like lower prices, the union, which demands higher wages, and the stockholder, who desires dividends and/or price appreciation. In this, what is important is that it gives firms the appearance of consciously seeking to attain certain objectives. It may be argued that in reality there is no identifiable decision-making entity—*the firm*. Instead, whatever actions are attributed to the firm actually result from the collective actions of individuals, and groups of individuals. In this sense, firms do not really have corporate-level objectives which guide the conduct of the individuals or groups of individuals who serve as decision makers. However, at times it is meaningful to assume that they do. In other words, analysis of firms may be facilitated by imparting to them a degree of rationality which, in fact, they do not really possess. For all practical purposes, one denies the existence of a rational decision-making entity called the firm, while at the same time he finds that this is a useful way of simplifying the analysis of a very complex system. Firms do not make decisions; corporations cannot have objectives. Assumptions to the contrary are made merely to facilitate analysis of the decision-making processes which take place in the world of business. These processes result in actions which are attributed to a lifeless, legal entity—the firm.

MANAGEMENT FUNCTIONS

In studying the process of decision-making within businesses, it turns out that regardless of product, market, or circumstances there are certain common activities in which firms engage as an inevitable consequence of being in operation. These have been termed *management functions*. These functional areas or common responsibilities may be isolated and studied almost as though they were separate and distinct disciplines. One common breakdown of business, or management, functions is as follows: marketing, production, and finance. To these we might add accounting, communications, personnel, research and development, or industrial relations. Regardless of length, no list of functions should be looked on as exhaustive. Ultimately, a firm's management is not so much concerned with specifying the functions themselves, as with being sure that these functions are carried out in as close to an optimal manner as possible.

It is in larger firms that functional specialization has been carried to its greatest extremes. It is easier to supervise people engaged in like or closely related activities, provided one's scale makes it economic to organize along such lines. Common identification with a particular function facilitates analysis of the manner in which that function is carried out. At the same time, this may lead to the development of a separate discipline with a language all its own. Functional specialization in business logically led to functional specialization in the teaching of business, and this further reinforced the development of the business functions as separate disciplines.

The various identifying labels which have been attached to business functions have become familiar to business students if only for the fact that traditionally they have had to elect a functionally identified major field of study. But a student, to a lesser or greater extent, is also expected to visualize the entire business scene, much as the owner or manager of a small business must. The latter lives intimately with all aspects of his business. From a functional standpoint he cannot become too specialized lest he emphasize some functions at the expense of others.

What is the significance of this sojourn into the world of the "obvious"? The point is that businesses are being run more and more by specialists, but not by *isolationists*. The firm is managed through a complex interaction of a variety of skills, but the conduct of these activities is meaningful and effective only when they are related to a definable direction in which the firm might move. In this respect a business firm may be likened to a simple biologic organism attempting to exist within some niche in a complex and basically hostile environment. A momentary abatement of the forces detrimental to its survival allows it to establish its initial foothold. After this, adaptation occurs so that it may better exist within its environment and prepare itself for whatever future threats might be foreseen to its survival. Under such circumstances, focus on any part or particular feature of the environment can be potentially as disastrous as placing overemphasis on the satisfactory performance of some of its life-sustaining functions to the detriment of others.

So it is with the modern business firm striving to exist within a complex economic environment. Behavior within the firm must in some manner be motivated by considerations of its effect on the firm as a whole. Again making use of the assumption that firms have goals or objectives, the danger exists that the direction a department or part of a firm takes may not be consistent with that direction which is best for the firm as a whole. To illustrate, let us look on the firm as combining the economists' traditional inputs of land, labor, and capital. Let us further assume that these inputs are freely variable and that the firm has a land department, a labor department, and a capital department. One possible way of organizing the firm's activities would be to specify that each department attempt to maximize its profits. Under such circumstances, assuming that each department is successful, maximum profits to the firm as a whole would dictate that the factors of production be allocated to the point that:

$$\frac{\text{Marginal productivity of land}}{\text{price of land}} = \frac{\text{Marginal productivity of labor}}{\text{price of labor}} =$$

$$\frac{\text{Marginal productivity of capital}}{\text{price of capital}}$$

If one assumes perfect competition in the factor markets, maximization of profitability by departments would also maximize profits for the firm as a whole. If, however, the efforts of one department to attain maximum profits from the manipulation of its inputs affect the price of inputs to another department, then coordination of the efforts of the separate departmental (or functional) managers is a prerequisite to optimum profits for the firm as a whole. And in fact, business firms have executive committee meetings and lines of communication established that perform exactly this function. In the smallest of firms, the one-man firm, such meetings and communication are constant even though at times a particular issue may be relatively singular in its scope—for example, how to measure income for the past fiscal year for tax purposes. In larger firms, a more formal mechanism is required: organization along functional lines.

THE FUNCTIONS OF MANAGEMENT
IN HISTORICAL PERSPECTIVE

Organizing business activities along functional lines is clearly a source of many problems. Why then, one might ask, is so much emphasis placed on the separate management functions? To answer this question requires some consideration of business history.

Narrowly viewing the historic evolution of one of the functions of business ignores the fact that what happens to a firm is the consequence of a series of decisions made in several functional areas. Business history can only be understood in terms of the stream of decisions made by firms, each seeking to optimize some measure of performance by manipulation of what they can control and by adaptation to an environment which at any point in time is largely given. With this in mind, let us briefly consider the manner in which emphasis given to the three principal functional fields by American business has changed over time. What follows is not offered as a capsule history of business finance, as is so often the case with introductory-textbook treatments. Instead, the intention is to supply the student with a brief historic analysis of the manner in which finance, marketing, and production considerations may at various points in time be related to the economy as a whole and to the then contemporary business scene. What is important is not the completeness of the historical treatment, but the approach taken.

The American Economy to the Turn of the Century

Prior to the Civil War, agriculture formed the base of the American economy. Rural and frontier families were of necessity forced to be largely self-sufficient, with the domestic market mechanism largely oriented to supplying the needs of the scattered centers of urban population. For manufactured goods, there was heavy reliance on foreign sources of supply. This made the wholesaler a major influence in the economy, although the functions of these early wholesalers were typically far more extensive than today. Wholesaling was commonly combined with importing, and also with retailing and manufacturing. Wholesalers played a key role in assembling and dispersing the increasing proportion of agricultural output sold on the open market.

These early wholesalers were also key financial intermediaries. They often supplied capital to the farmer or manufacturer in advance of production while at the same time carrying retailers until their goods were sold to final customers.

After the Civil War the United States found itself a nation with a rapidly increasing population and an expanding domestic industrial base. With the change from home to factory production the wholesaler still remained a key distributive intermediary, but his functions changed. The last half of the nineteenth century has been characterized as the period during which wholesalers turned from general to specialized operations.[1] Thus, dry-goods wholesalers were replaced by those separately carrying notions, linens, silk goods, hats, hosiery, etc. This period saw the gradual divorcement of wholesaling from importing, manufacturing, and retailing. However, the independent wholesaler still remained the principal outlet for the production of an increasingly large-scale manufacturing sector. Wholesalers linked manufacturing to consumer markets which were both scattered and concentrated. The scale of many early wholesalers was quite large. For example, by 1856 there were some 200 wholesalers and jobbing houses in Boston alone which sold shoes and whose annual business probably exceeded $50 million.[2]

The latter half of the nineteenth century also saw significant developments in production and finance, and the manner in which decisions in these areas were made by the firm. As population and purchasing power increased so did pressure on the manufacturing sector to supply standardized, mass-produced goods for what was essentially a sellers' market. This forced many firms to the realization that profitability was directly related to their ability

---

[1] Theodore N. Beckman and Nathanael H. Engle, *Wholesaling: Principles and Practice.* 3rd ed. (New York: Ronald Press, Inc., 1959), pp. 71–72.
[2] *Ibid.,* p. 73.

to remove production constraints and hence to spread fixed costs over larger volumes of output. The influence of production managers and engineers was felt at the highest corporate decision-making levels.

This was also the heyday of the large-scale financier. Unhampered by effective antitrust legislation, financially-oriented executives were free to explore the profit possibilities of a wide variety of forms of business organization, many of them involving control over large blocks of capital and productive capacity. The lure of large and quick rewards drew capital and entrepreneurship into a business world in which special privilege, ruthless competition, and cyclical instability were not unknown.

At the turn of the century, for many firms the finance function was managed on two corporate levels. Overall financial planning was typically the concern of top management. Additionally, a financial executive was frequently found on the same organizational level as manufacturing, with both reporting to a general manager. The financial manager's main concern was with cash flow, and this often led to his having significant influence in the revenue-generating and expense areas of sales and advertising. However, the scope of his influence was limited. Generally there was little he could do to control the environment within which he operated, with the final decision as to the core idea and total pattern of resource commitment typically made at higher levels. Large as some firms became, dominant individuals or small groups were often able to effectively guide their destiny.

Through World War I

Even though the pioneering research of Frederick W. Taylor antedated the turn of the century, it was in the period through World War I that scientific management made its greatest impact. Although the term scientific management is most commonly applied to Taylor's work, in actuality there were a series of contributors all of whom were concerned with the analysis of mass production processes and their more efficient organization.[3] Scientific management aimed at the attainment of the economies of scale through specialization. Jobs were divided into their various components in the hope that more efficient combinations of effort could be discovered. Concise and detailed written instructions were developed to describe how specific jobs were to be carried out in relation to other jobs and to the overall production process. Ostensibly this increased the emphasis given to production manage-

---

[3]E. Brech and L. Urwick, *The Making of Scientific Management: Thirteen Pioneers.* Vol. I (London: Management Publications Trust, 1949).

ment. However, scientific management, by dividing the manufacturing process into identifiable stages, made it easier for the financial manager to determine and control the costs of production.

Increases in the scale of production also affected the distributive sector. A direct effect was that as markets increased in size so did the interest of manufacturers in the manner in which they were serviced. As the application of the principles of scientific management served to further exhaust production economies, it was logical that manufacturers should consider the benefits that might be realized by their taking over the responsibility for the marketing of their products—by eliminating the wholesaler and engaging in direct distribution.

The dependence of manufacturers on the independent wholesaler diminished for yet another reason, stated by Cox as follows:

> [Wholesalers'] commanding position in individual markets was frequently reinforced by their importance as channels through which retailers and manufacturers obtained access to the money markets. Their financial dominance broke down when many retailers and manufacturers grew large enough to go direct to the money market themselves.[4]

Between the Wars

Pent-up consumer demand from World War I helped fuel the industrial expansion of the 1920's. The climb upward was far from steady, especially for many firms whose expansion had resulted in working capital being devoted to the payment of interest and dividends. The sharp rise in prices and inventory recession of 1920–21 strained the capital structure of many firms, especially those heavily dependent on the consumer sector. For example, in 1921 it took a pledge of $20 million of the private fortune of Julius Rosenwald to keep Sears, Roebuck and Company from bankruptcy. This was notwithstanding the fact that Sears' sales had increased from approximately $182 million in 1918 to a record $250 million in 1920.[5]

Economic recovery in the latter years of the decade helped focus attention of corporations and individuals on the securities markets. This led to misplaced emphasis on the financial manager's role as an investment banker. In practice it overlooked the operational importance of problems of internal

[4]Reavis Cox, Charles S. Goodman and Thomas C. Fichandler, *Distribution in a High Level Economy* (Englewood Cliffs, N.J.: Prentice-Hall, Inc., 1965), p. 52.

[5]Boris Emmet and John E. Jeuck, *Catalogues and Counters: A History of Sears, Roebuck and Company* (Chicago: University of Chicago Press, 1950), pp. 211–215.

financial management. Internally, the viewpoint taken was quite narrow and heavily concerned with budgetary control—identification, tracing and control of costs through detailed records-keeping activity. The objective was to keep costs within predetermined limits. This control was a logical outgrowth of scientific management.

Despite much concern over the role that wholesalers played in the economy, in relative terms the wholesale sector did not materially lose ground to direct distribution. Merchant wholesalers were reported as accounting for approximately two-fifths of all wholesale sales in every business census taken during the 1920's and 1930's. When the wholesaler was displaced it was selectively, i.e., only certain types of goods or industries were affected. Furthermore, losses in some wholesalers' lines were offset by gains in others. Some wholesalers reacted to threats to their position by taking a revitalized approach to selling and through the realization of operating economies. Others fought a generally losing battle for channel control by resorting to such practices as blacklisting, price maintenance, "fair" practice codes, price fixing, and the like.

Regardless of its effect on the wholesale sector, there was a marked increase in the interest of manufacturers in the markets for their goods and services. Improvements in mass-communication media gave sellers the ability to influence demand and to "pull" products through the channel of distribution. Even though many producers were reluctant to engage in contracyclical advertising during the Depression, general recognition did develop of the fact that demand need no longer be accepted as "given." This led firms to think in terms of the whole spectrum of revenue-cost-volume possibilities which could be generated by changes in the amounts spent on advertising and personal selling.

Finally, it is meaningful to note that during the Depression many firms found that external financial intermediaries were increasingly becoming involved in the day-to-day management of their financial affairs. Banks unwillingly found themselves in partnerships with faltering concerns plagued by liquidity problems. Indebtedness of clients forced bank officers to take an active interest in their affairs. This involvement took on many forms, a common one being membership on the board of directors.

World War II to the Present

During World War II, strength in the industrial-goods sector, and an only partially satisfied consumer-goods market, helped alleviate the liquidity problems which many businesses faced as a consequence of the Depression.

American success in the war was in no small way related to the domestic production base which supported overseas military operations. While the war created substantial pent-up demand for consumer goods, it also resulted in materially expanded production capacity. The war saw not only the forced-draft development of technology, but also gave stimulus to the development of better methods—for example, linear programming, for organizing production processes.

While the widely anticipated postwar depression never materialized, it did become apparent that the war (postwar expectations to the contrary) had generated excess capacity in many firms and industries. An emerging interest developed in the nature of markets and in the analysis of demand.

The decentralization movement following World War II significantly affected the management of the business functions. As a series of scattered but concentrated urban markets developed, it became apparent that in many cases there were material advantages to be realized by serving such markets on a regional basis. The ensuing geographic dispersion of operating units necessitated widespread delegation of authority. In order to react to fast-changing market conditions and compete effectively, autonomous management within broad limits of corporate policy was vital. The finance function was expanded beyond its normal concern with operational budgetary control to include concern with the future. New prestige became the lot of the financial manager. He was not only responsible for day-to-day financial control made more complex by virtue of decentralization but in many cases he came to share with top management the responsibility for determining the future course of company events.

The Role of the Finance Manager

The finance function now attained the same organizational level as the other functional departments. In addition, its corporate presence was often extended by personal representation on top-management committees at presidential and board of director levels. But, it was still a function with two discrete corporate identities—one tied to decision making, the other to organizational housekeeping.

The housekeeping function benefitted materially from research directed at the application of electronic data processing to business activities. By providing a capacity for "real time" or instantaneous reporting, by enabling the generation of reports encompassing even the most Lilliputian cost activity, by facilitating the accumulation, analysis, and storage of each and every bit of corporate data, the computer began to transform control and record-keeping from a burdensome, complex activity to one performed with perfunctory precision.

As a consequence, the decision-making aspects of finance have received the greatest attention in recent years. If the financial manager is looked on as being on the same level organizationally with the marketing and production managers, and if all three make decisions and plans capable of affecting the firm's destiny, clearly there must be a coordination of their efforts. Furthermore, a mechanism must be established for moderating disputes and resolving differences of opinion. With this in mind, let us briefly examine changes in the decision-making roles defined for marketing and production executives in the post-World War II period.

The Role of the Marketing Manager

Excess capacity and heightened competition forced on business firms the necessity for analyzing, adapting to, and influencing the market for their products. This eventually caused them to do something concrete about implementing what otherwise might be termed a lofty objective. In the late 1950's there developed the "consumer-oriented," "total marketing," or "marketing management" concept. The key factor in making such approaches operational is summarized by Howard as follows:

> Marketing management is that area of company management having to do with the broad problem of sales . . . it implies an integration of the various marketing activities and a downward delegation of authority.[6]

The central idea is that marketing considerations are allowed to affect a whole family of decisions which in the past, in terms of the traditional separation of the business functions, were thought of as being outside of, or peripheral to, marketing—that is, could be made independently of consumer demand considerations. The key word in the paragraph quoted above is *integration,* the process whereby the firm develops a marketing strategy. Strategy in this sense may be defined as the complete spectrum of responses a firm might be expected to make to actual and projected marketing alternatives.

Thinking in strategic terms forces one to consider both sequence and timing. Development of a strategy necessarily involves an estimate of the various future states of affairs which might be encountered by a firm, together

---

[6]John A. Howard, *Marketing Management: Analysis and Decision* (Homewood, Ill.: Richard D. Irwin, Inc., 1957), p. 3.

with the specification of the corresponding responses the firm will make given its basic utility function or corporate objective.

The marketing management concept argues that a compelling reason exists for giving the marketing executive a strong if not dominant voice in strategy formulation. The justification offered is simple: the marketing executive is the closest of any to the consumer, and it is to the consumer and the market that the corporation's entire activity is directed. In this sense the marketing executive is looked on as the final coordinator of the firm's activities. Organizationally, he may be on a par with executives in production and finance, but in the event of disputes among functional areas it is maintained that his opinion is affected by consumer-demand considerations to a degree that the others are not. The marketing executive's role in decision making, it is argued, should be elevated by virtue of the fact that he represents the firm's customers or its market. It is for the market that costs are incurred and from which revenues are generated.

The Role of the Production Manager

The post-World War II period also saw changes in the decision-making role of the production manager. Increases in the complexity of products and production processes dictated that managers in this area become increasingly knowledgeable with respect to technology. In many industries, research and development assumed such critical importance as to warrant establishment as a separate activity of the firm, often organizationally divorced from line production. Additionally, there was the impact of the computer. Many production managers had to face the necessity of retraining in this area or the prospect of being forced to blindly rely on specialized staff assistants capable of materially affecting the production process. Computers found a wide series of applications, ranging all the way from production programming and quality control to operations research.

Even though the production manager may formally be charged with a significant portion of the total expenses incurred by a firm, there are definite limits to his ability to make resource-allocation decisions. In other words, the production manager is expected to maximize output and minimize cost within general guidelines. Even though he may participate in the establishment of these guidelines, he is not looked on as having the final word and is expected to subordinate his own interests so as to coincide with those of the firm in general.

Recent literature in the production management area emphasizes the involvement of the production executive in what amounts to resource allocation decisions. Garrett and Silver term this taking an "overall, or systems, view-point," in which:

> The entire firm is viewed as a single operating system and is considered to be the appropriate arena for problem solving. When a problem arises, it is examined with regard to the total firm rather than just in terms of the sector that is apparently involved. The objective of this approach is to identify all significant interactions between the problem area and the operation of the firm as a whole. Thus, it is hoped that decision making in any functional area, such as the production control department, will reflect what is best for the company.[7]

At the same time that some have defined an expanded role for the production manager, it has been suggested by others that his authority should be somewhat less than absolute with respect to the products he produces or could produce. The marketing manager is often given a voice in the former, while marketing research and research and development in many cases exercise no small amount of influence over what might be produced.

SUMMARY AND CONCLUSIONS

In summary, a record period of peacetime economic expansion in the early 1960's afforded many business firms the opportunity to search out an appropriate balance of responsibilities among managers in the three major functional areas. This internal realignment of responsibilities was accomplished during a time when liquidity was not a major issue and when there was generally easy and favorable access to sources of external financing. Both factors served to reduce the involvement of the financial manager with his traditionally most important responsibilities and allowed him to extend his abilities to the areas of future planning and resource allocation. This evolution of the finance function occurred at a time when the responsibilities of marketing and production managers were also undergoing considerable revision.

One thing should be clear from this brief historical analysis. If there is a direction in which the traditional business functions have been redefined it has been in terms of responsible executives taking a broader view of the firm's activities. The collapse of the former narrow pattern of specialization was

---

[7]Leonard J. Garrett and Milton Silver, *Production Management Analysis* (New York: Harcourt, Brace & World, Inc., 1965), p. 65.

not without possibilities for duplication of responsibility and potential conflict. This forces on managers in the various functional areas the necessity for liaison and cooperation, and clearly validates the wisdom of having procedures established to mediate disputes and reduce conflict to reasonable proportions.

Historically, business management has been broken down into a series of arbitrarily defined functions. These consist of grouped activities commonly looked on as being the inevitable consequence of business operations. While the functional view has been a useful one for teaching purposes and has served satisfactorily as a basis for departmentalization, organization by function in the business world can and does lead to intrafirm conflict and a suboptimal pattern of corporate-resource allocation. A major concern of modern organization theory is with the interrelated nature of decisions made in the separate functional areas. The so-called "systemic" approach to management, discussed previously, calls for the total adaptation of a business firm to its environment. The firm is looked on as an operating system in competition with other such operating systems. Instead of starting with a model of business operations which assumes that certain activities should be commonly grouped, the attempt is made to define a model appropriate to the particular changing pattern of influences which may affect the firm's destiny. Not ignored in the process are the indirect and conceivably undesirable side effects of decisions made in order to achieve certain definable objectives.

The view taken of the financial manager's job in this book is consistent with such an approach to business management. However, it is impossible to define a decision-making role for the financial manager, or any other manager, without paying some attention to the manner in which his role correctly or incorrectly may have been defined in the past. Defining the financial manager's role in systemic terms leads to a constant comparison with the roles traditionally defined for him in the past. The "new" financial manager is much more concerned with decision making and resource allocation than was his historic counterpart. However, taking a systemic view still does not result in his being *the* single, all-powerful decision-making entity within the firm. Even more so than in the functionally oriented firm, there is a real need for top management. Top management is responsible for the definition of the core idea and for leading activities toward a profitable exploitation of that core idea. The role of top management is to anticipate and otherwise moderate tendencies toward suboptimization which must arise as the consequence of splitting up the responsibilities for direction of an enterprise beyond the managerial capabilities of a single person. Redefinition of the financial manager's job in systemic terms is designed to minimize the effects of conflict and to moderate tendencies toward suboptimization. It cannot eliminate them altogether.

Business education is gradually being forced to move in the direction of collapsing the functional fields, if only for the fact that such a trend is clearly established in the contemporary business scene. The single most important objective of this book is to permit students to integrate work in the various functional areas, and in the process to study the finance function in relationship to the total pattern of firm decision making.

SUGGESTED REFERENCES

Brech, E., and L. Urwick, *The Making of Scientific Management: Thirteen Pioneers*, Vol. I. London: Management Publications Trust, 1949.

Buffa, Elwood, *Modern Production Management*. New York: John Wiley & Sons, Inc., 1965.

Cox, Reavis, Charles S. Goodman, and Thomas C. Fichandler, *Distribution in a High Level Economy*. Englewood Cliffs, N.J.: Prentice-Hall, Inc., 1965.

Dewing, Arthur S., *The Financial Policy of Corporations*. New York: Ronald Press, Inc., 1920.

Garrett, Leonard J., and Milton Silver, *Production Management Analysis*. New York: Harcourt, Brace & World, Inc., 1965.

Howard, John A., *Marketing Management: Analysis and Planning*. Rev. ed. Homewood, Ill.: Richard D. Irwin, Inc., 1963.

Levy, Lester S., and Roy J. Sampson, *American Economic Development: Growth of the U.S. in the Western World*. Boston: Allyn and Bacon, Inc., 1962.

Revzan, David A., *Wholesaling in Marketing Organization*. New York: John Wiley & Sons, Inc., 1961.

Starr, Martin K., *Production Management: Systems and Synthesis*. Englewood Cliffs, N.J.: Prentice-Hall, Inc., 1964.

Weston, J. Fred, *The Scope and Methodology of Finance*. Englewood Cliffs, N.J.: Prentice-Hall, Inc., 1966.

Administration of the Finance Function

Good order is the foundation of all good things.
—Edmund Burke

In this chapter we discuss organizational arrangements developed by business firms to facilitate the administration of the finance function. The illustrations are all concerned with very large corporations. From them one can reasonably generalize to most medium-size and even smaller-size firms organized along formal lines. But our conclusions should not be extended in unqualified fashion to very small firms, especially those that are owner-operated. In that event, finance, marketing, and production decisions are likely to be made by one individual or by a small, closely knit group. The lack of formal organization or the very loose organization which frequently characterizes such firms makes it difficult to identify, let alone analyze, how the finance function is administered.

BUSINESS ORGANIZATION

Such a wide range of organizational structures is found among contemporary American business firms that one may wonder whether it is possible to meaningfully generalize in this respect. One way to give some order to the discussion is to attempt to relate various types of organizational structures to the situations in which they exist. It is clear that many factors influence organizational structure. Let us look at five: legal form of organization, age and size of firm, geographical outreach, diversity of firm, and degree of centralization.

Legal Form of Organization

Corporate bylaws usually specify that a firm appoint *at a minimum* four officers: president, vice-president, secretary and treasurer (with the latter two offices sometimes held by the same person). While the majority of businesses in the United States are not incorporated, it cannot be denied that their organization is affected by the corporate model. Furthermore, the four offices cited have become standard for almost any type of organized activity, whether profit-oriented or not.

Thus, even though firms cannot usually avoid carrying out certain common activities or functions, the heart of their formal organization is four job titles, only one of which—the treasurer—is directly related to any one of the three basic functions, finance. The simplest way of expanding the organization chart to take account of this is shown in Figure 3-1.[1]

Figure 3-1
Simple Functional Organization

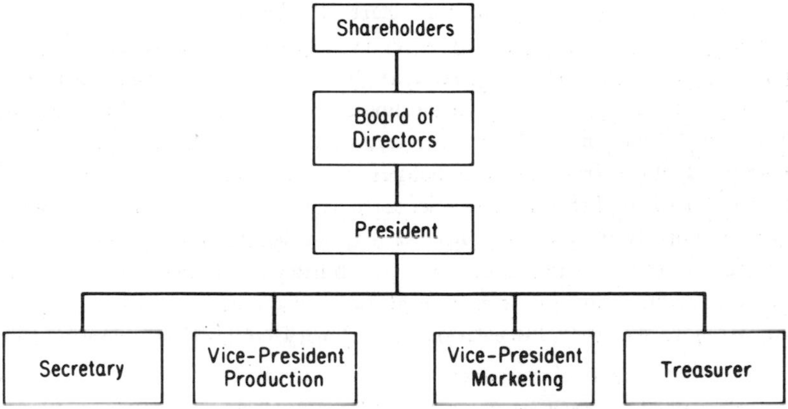

Simple functional organization positions the president between the board of directors, who are concerned with the firm's core idea and its development, and those concerned with the functions which are basic to the enterprise. Very little attention should be paid to the titles of the executives in Figure 3-1. The production and the marketing managers need not be at the vice-presidential level, and the financial manager, as we shall see, may be identified by a great many different titles. The important thing to note about simple functional organization is that it represents an attempt to attain the advantages of specialization. This is done by identifying those activities (functions) which are central to the ability of the firm to exploit its core idea, and to commonly group persons engaged in carrying out those activities.

Age and Size of Firm

It may be argued that the simple functional organization does not represent an accurate picture of the managerial structure of a firm which has been in business very long, or which is of any significant size. Let us consider how age and size *jointly* affect organizational structure. This recognizes that

[1]Subsequent organizational charts omit the shareholders and the board of directors.

the two are so frequently correlated that consideration of the separate effects of each would be inappropriate.

With growth and size, the president and the principal officers can no longer give personal attention to all the details involved in managing the firm. This leads to possibly unwanted but inevitable dependence on others. First comes the delegation of operational responsibilities to operating departments. Then—and these events may occur simultaneously—it is to be expected that staff departments will develop to assist both the corporate officials in the management of the firm, and the operating departments in the integration, supervision, and performance of the firm's operational activities. Thus there occurs a filling out of the organization chart (Figure 3-2).

Notice that the treasurer and secretary are depicted on a separate level above the management staff departments. Should they be considered line or staff? A great deal has been written on line-staff relationships and the flow of authority in business firms. Line authority, which supposedly carries the right to command, flows from the shareholders, through their elected representatives, the board of directors, and thence to the president. After that, what happens is not always clear nor necessarily revealed through simple analysis of the formal organization. Numerous possibilities are to be found, ranging all the way from almost no delegation of authority (the centralized, authoritarian firm) to widespread delegation of authority coupled with consultation

Figure 3-2
Management and Operating Departments With Supporting Staff

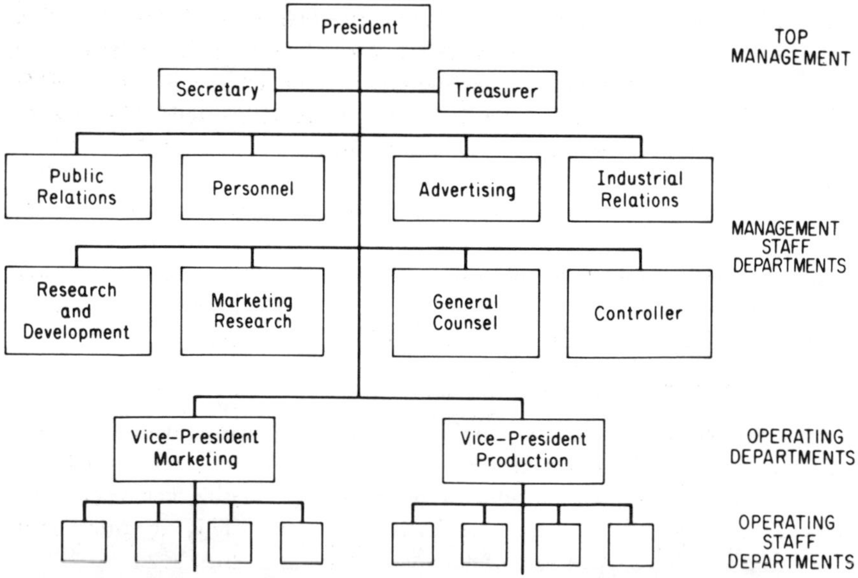

in its use (the decentralized, democratic firm). Probably the greatest problems are encountered in trying to identify the authority possessed by staff groups, and in distinguishing those who occupy line positions from those who occupy staff positions. Because of his concern with liquidity, which is essential to corporate survival, it is likely that the treasurer (or the principal financial officer but with some other title) will exercise line authority in the area of finance. Finances are critical to the viability of the entire system, and if organizational survival is threatened time may be lacking to seek consultation. This leads to the conclusion that most firms will position a chief financial officer somewhere in the line organization.

In Figure 3-2, determination of the treasurer's authority is not facilitated by the mirror-image positioning of the secretary in the organization chart. Both are corporate officers, and both are usually board members, or have close working relations with the board. However, the secretary's basic responsibilities are in the organization and reporting of the board's activities. The secretary's knowledge of board actions frequently may make him an important *source* of corporate policy, but the positioning does not usually have line authority in the carrying out of board policies. One possible exception is when the secretary's duties revolving around the board constitute a less than full-time commitment, and he is assigned additional responsibilities as a consequence.

A Question of Titles

In this chapter we consider only organizational structures that represent basically different possibilities for the administration of the finance function. Proliferation of corporate titles and a lack of consistency in the use of existing titles make this a difficult task. For example, J. Fred Weston's study of 59 large firms showed that the responsibility for the administration of the finance function was vested in the following individuals:[2]

Title	Number of Companies
Treasurer	23
Vice-president, finance	10
Vice-president, treasurer	7
Treasurer, controller	5
Vice-president, finance-treasurer	4
Treasurer-secretary	4
Executive vice-president	2
Vice-president-controller	2
President	1
Vice-president	1
Total	59

[2]J. Fred Weston, "The Finance Function," *Journal of Finance,* 9 (September 1954), p. 268.

One common source of confusion is between the titles *treasurer* and *controller*. The treasurer is the official of the corporation held responsible for its funds. In addition to being an agent of trust he is usually concerned with the planning and maintenance of overall liquidity, and with the development of an optimal financial structure for the firm. The controller, on the other hand, is usually less involved in financial management and planning, but is more concerned with the actual disbursement of and accounting for funds. Often the controller's principal concern is with the administration of budgets—that is, in seeing that the firm's resources are managed in accordance with a predetermined plan. Thus if this is his role, the performance of his duties is facilitated by positioning him closer to the operating departments, where disbursements are being made and funds received, than to top management where policy is being made and implemented. In positioning the treasurer and the controller in the organization chart, Fox suggests one approach which is to be respected for the soundness of its logic and its apparent ease of application:

> If either the controller or treasurer is regarded as the chief financial officer of the company . . . then one should report to the other and the superior should report to the president. If both are competent and there is insufficient justification for the retention of a chief financial officer to whom both would report, the controller and the treasurer should report directly to the president.[3]

The important issue here is not where the treasurer and the controller are positioned in the organization chart, but with the logical placement of individuals within the corporate hierarchy taking account of their responsibilities. In the top-level administration of the finance function a great many organizational arrangements are found in practice, a representative sample of which are depicted in Figure 3-3. Without reference to the job descriptions supporting the position titles it is extremely difficult in some cases to determine how financial management is really accomplished in the firms pictured. Whether companies have treasurers, controllers, financial vice-presidents, chief accountants, or general auditors is not clearly related to any single factor such as size, age, or geographic outreach, although it cannot be denied that fragmented responsibility for the administration of the finance function is not characteristic of very small firms.

A great many different arrangements seem to be feasible, even preferred,

---

[3]William M. Fox, *The Management Process* (Homewood, Ill.: Richard D. Irwin, Inc., 1963), p. 260.

Figure 3-3
Administration of the Finance Function
Some Representative Organizational Structures

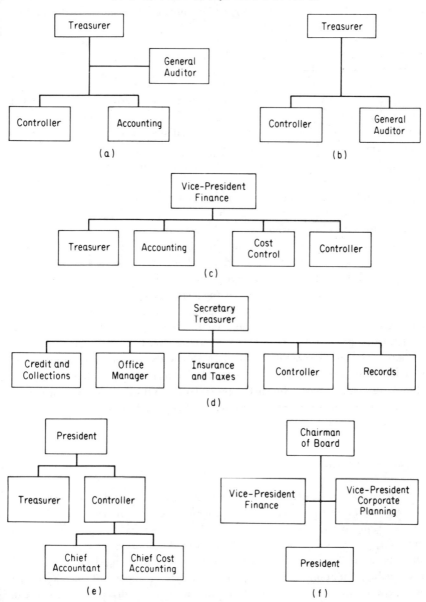

in firms in quite similar circumstances. One possible source of difficulty in this respect may be the tendency many firms have to fit positions to individuals, rather than the reverse. Thus the controller's position may be strengthened in a firm with a weak treasurer, or the position of financial vice-president may be added for the same reason.

Geographical Outreach

Frequently firms with operations covering a wide geographic area find it practical to depart from a system of functional organization in favor of one which better recognizes the degree of physical separation between their far-flung operational units. Clearly, this type of divisional organization implies a certain degree of decentralization. A geographic arrangement reflecting a high degree of divisional autonomy is pictured in Figure 3-4. Here parallel organization structures are to be found in the territorial divisions, with a finance, production, and marketing manager assigned to each. If the divisions are to enjoy autonomy, line authority would extend from the treasurer, down through the executive vice-president, and thence through the divisional vice-president (and there would be no dotted lines in Figure 3-4). Instead we have indicated the alternate arrangement, one that involves to a lesser or greater extent direct contact between the principal financial officer, the treasurer, and the finance managers in the operating divisions. Even under autonomy, there would probably be some contact between the headquarters and field finance personnel; the key is the extent to which the former exercise authority over the latter. The danger in this is that the divisional managers may find themselves nominally accountable for performance, but actions from above over which they have little control may influence that performance. Frequently the time required for review and approval of divisional actions is a critical point of contention.

Diversity of Firm

Often the degree of diversity of a firm has a greater influence on organizational structure than mere size or geographic extent of operations. Thus a firm's organization may be forced to take account of extreme diversity in products, processes, customers, or channels of distribution. Diversity is probably the greatest practical deterrent to organization along functional lines. Presumably, functional organization fosters the grouping of like activities and permits economies of specialization. However, a diverse operation can

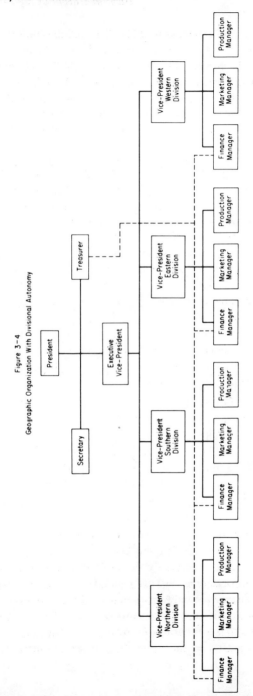

Figure 3-4
Geographic Organization With Divisional Autonomy

create marketing and production departments which have little in common and among which there is little in the way of transferable knowledge.

The finance function is the one least affected by diversity. Even though the activities conducted in two operating divisions may differ greatly, there still remains the essential problem of reducing their operations to their financial equivalents. Furthermore, unless activities are turned into dollar values in some reasonably consistent manner, one does not obtain an accurate picture of the total firm's activities. If a very diverse firm is to be organized into profit centers, some common agreement will have to be obtained as to the allocation of costs, with fixed-cost loadings being the critical factor. For this reason, a marketing and production organization that reflects a firm's diversity may be possible only if the finance function is handled on a far more uniform basis and at a management level well above divisional organization units.

Degree of Centralization

From the above discussion one may infer that the finance function is the least amenable of the three to decentralization. If this were not so there would be no real financial control. Frequently, policy manuals and operating procedures limit the ability of divisional managers to make expenditures or encumber the firm, either by specifying dollar limits to individual transactions and/or by requiring corporate approval of all capital construction. Even in cases where divisional managers are given complete freedom in the types of expenditures they may make, they are still audited and their authority is defined within budgetary limits.

It should be noted that the computer is a powerful aid to management in recentralizing the finance function, if this is felt desirable. The computer facilitates the development and administration of detailed budgetary standards applied to a very large number of operating units. Additionally, it provides for timely reporting of data evaluating performance against established standards. Thus if some of the decentralization of American business firms in the post-World War II period, especially in the financial area, is looked on as unavoidable but not necessarily desirable, the development of computerized total-firm information systems could facilitate a substantial degree of recentralization in business organization.

Specific organizational arrangements can also facilitate centralized administration of the finance function, even in firms very large in size and very diverse in their activities. Let us study one arrangement used by General

Figure 3-5
Top Financial Staff Organization at General Motors

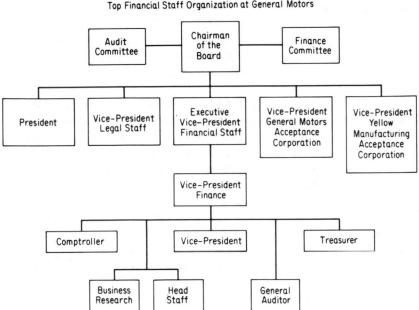

Source: William M. Fox, The Management Process, (Homewood, Ill.: Richard D. Irwin, Inc., 1963), pp. 261, 331.

Motors (Figure 3-5) [4] Here the chairman of the board is the chief executive officer of the corporation. He also acts as chairman of the finance committee of the board, and serves as a member of the executive committee. The finance committee works closely with the executive committee, which is headed by the president. Between them, these two committees receive the delegated power of the board to determine and implement the financial policies of the corporation. The finance committee consists of 11 members. In addition to the chairman of the board, there are three management members (the president, the operational staff and financial staff executive vice-presidents), and six nonmanagement members, with all members of the finance committee also being members of the board of directors.

Given the power of the finance committee and its close association with

---

[4]For a description of General Motors organizational practices, see Fox, *op. cit.*, pp. 260–261. Not shown are three executive vice-presidents reporting to the president, two of which head up the principal operating divisions of the company.

the executive committee, how much authority do the division managers possess? Fox concludes as follows:

> Subject to company-wide policy and reporting constraints and the centralization of certain activities, the general manager acts much like the president of an independent firm.[5]

Overall resource allocation is determined at a level above the president, but on the other hand he is a participant in the process. The authority of the board in this respect is acknowledged by the corporate model of organization. Perhaps what stands out here is that the organizational structure of General Motors is designed to make this authority an effective influence on the company's operations. The operating divisions are subject to audit by the central controller's staff.

The key operational element in the General Motors plan is that it permits selective decentralization of some functions and centralized retention of others. The General Motors example is cited not so much for its general relevance as for its being indicative that effective top-management and shareholder control over the finance function is not necessarily precluded by giant size or diversity of activities.

ADMINISTRATION OF THE FINANCE FUNCTION: FOUR CASE STUDIES

To illustrate the manner in which the finance function is administered in practice, we reproduce below several organization charts. Those chosen are merely illustrative; in no way is this intended to be a representative sample, although a merchandising firm, a public utility, an industrial firm and an insurance company are included. All the companies chosen are large by any set of standards.

Sears, Roebuck and Company

While organization charts traditionally depict formal reporting channels and the flow of authority, the one pictured for Sears, Roebuck and Company (Figure 3-6) is more descriptive of the group of personnel which collectively might be termed "top management." One's first impression of this organization chart might well be that an unusually large number of executives report

---

[5]*Ibid.,* pp. 327, 329.

Figure 3-6

Organizational Relationships Sears, Roebuck and Company

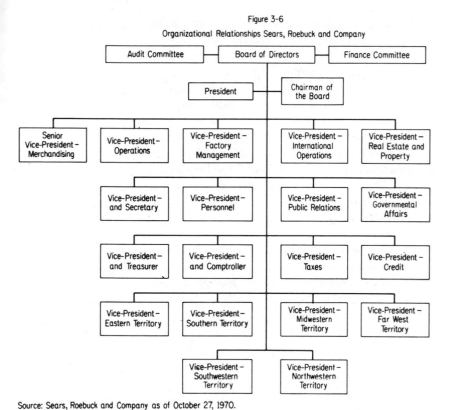

Source: Sears, Roebuck and Company as of October 27, 1970.

to the president and the board chairman. In this respect, the comments of a 1950 history of this firm are worth noting.

> In formulating and executing its organization pattern, the company not only has paid little heed but has actually run counter to one of the favorite tenets of modern management theory—the "span of control," which seeks to limit the number of subordinates reporting to a single individual in order that that individual may exercise the detailed direction and control generally believed essential. In flouting this concept and in building a "broad" or "flat" organization instead of a "vertical" or "tall" organization, Sears, Roebuck has deliberately given each key executive so many assistants that it is impossible for him to exercise very close supervision over their activities.[6]

[6]Boris Emmet and John E. Jeuck, *Catalogues and Counters: A History of Sears, Roebuck and Company* (Chicago and London: The University of Chicago Press, 1950), p. 675.

Insofar as fiscal policy is concerned, two committees of the Board of Directors are involved: the Finance Committee in the establishment of policy and the Audit Committee in determining that operations are indeed carried out along predetermined lines.

Administration of the finance function is the primary responsibility of four vice-presidents. The Vice-President and Treasurer is responsible for cashiering and the internal handling of funds. This is no small charge in a firm which as of January 31, 1970 reported some $223 million in cash on hand, and which for the year ending on the same date reported sales of $8.9 billion. The Vice-President and Treasurer also handles a number of other fiscal responsibilities, including those which involve stockholders and the external money markets. An important concern in this area has to be five series of debentures due from 1972 to 1993 and which comprise the firm's long-term debt of $455 million.

The Vice-President and Comptroller's responsibilities center around internal accounting and auditing. The split of duties between the two executives above corresponds to one common pattern discussed previously.

In the year 1969 Sears paid $397 million in Federal and State income taxes. Therefore, the presence of an executive concerned with taxes at the highest policy-making level is not surprising. Finally, Sears' year-end position in 1969 found the firm with some $3.5 billion outstanding in customer installment accounts, equivalent to 40 percent of annual sales. Clearly, the fact that credit policy has a significant effect on both costs and revenues dictates top-level concern with this aspect of financial management.

In evaluating the strengths and weaknesses of the Sears' organizational plan, two additional considerations may prove useful to the reader. First, and this is not apparent from the chart, the effective coordination of the efforts of the executive team rests not on supervision down the line, but is accomplished by a number of working committees which group the key executives into a number of problem-oriented configurations. For example, in setting policy and defining administrative procedures in the credit area, the Vice-President for Credit is aided by the Credit Policy Committee, of which he is the chairman.

Second, the executives discussed to this point are aided by staffs of no small size. For example, there are presently 8 assistant comptrollers and 6 assistant treasurers. It is through such sub-organization that uniform fiscal policies must be defined to govern the operations of 826 retail stores, 11 catalog order plants, and 2,131 catalog, retail and telephone sales offices and independent catalog merchants. While the above overview of Sears' top-level financial management structure is oversimplified, the magnitude and complexity of the operation it controls cannot be understated.

Southern California Edison

At the time the organization charts for this large southern California company were current, they were engaged in the distribution of electricity to an area of some 65,000 square miles, inhabited by more than seven million people. As of December 31, 1968, the company had perpetual franchises to supply electricity for lighting to 16 counties and 152 cities and 630 unincorporated communities, the three largest cities served being Long Beach, Torrance, and Santa Ana. To meet this demand the company owned and operated 13 gas-and-oil fueled plants, 36 hydroelectric plants, and one nuclear generating station. To deliver their output some 9,000 miles of transmission lines were required.

In its organization, one finds a logical split between financial management and planning and the day-to-day accounting for this company's vast operations. The former is organized under the treasurer. The stress on planning is not illogical, inasmuch as the company serves one of the fastest-growing, fastest-changing areas of the country. Notice also the high-level recognition of the importance of taxation within the treasurer's organization (Figure 3-7).

It is in the comptroller's office (Figure 3-8) that we find organizational recognition of the complex nature of the company's operations. Clearly, customer accounting is a major problem for a firm which at the time serviced more than 2.3 million customers, some 2 million of them residential, making total payments of more than $580 million. On the other hand, the day to day management of disbursements is another major problem afforded high-level recognition in the way the company is organized. For example, in 1968 payments of more than $118 million were made to the company's more than 10,000 employees.

Finally, Southern California Edison's financial organization reflects the magnitude of its information needs and the manner in which they are met. In this respect it is interesting to note that a supervisor of statistical analysis appears on the same corporate level as the assistant controller-information systems. This formally recognizes that the analysis of data is at least as important as the data itself.

International Business Machines

We might argue that only through the use of its own computing equipment is it possible for a firm as large as the present-day International Business Machines Corporation to exercise reasonable financial control. In 1968

Figure 3-7

Southern California Edison Company, Organization of the Comptroller's Department

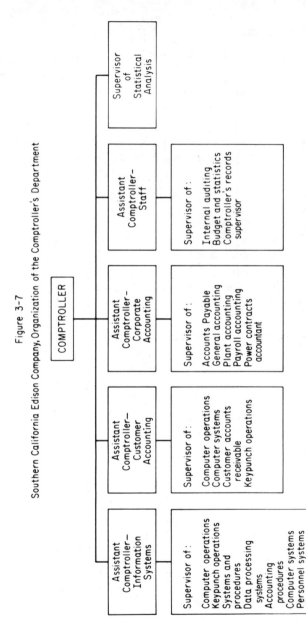

Source: Southern California Edison Company Organization chart as of March 13, 1967

Figure 3-8

Southern California Edison Company, Organization of the Treasurer's Department.

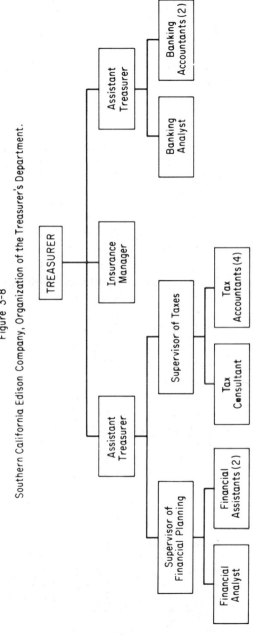

Sources: Southern California Edison Company Organizational Chart as of March 13, 1967

Figure 3-9
IBM Corporate Staff; Finance Staff

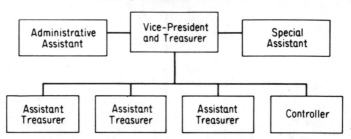

Source: International Business Machines Corporation, November 1966

this company's worldwide investment in plant, equipment, and rental machines was in excess of $3.4 billion; its annual sales and revenues totaled nearly $6.9 billion. In its financial organization there are three assistant treasurers and one controller reporting to the vice-president and treasurer (combined office), as shown in Figure 3-9. The first assistant treasurer (Figure 3-10) is concerned with overall financial management and business policy, presumably on something other than a day-to-day basis. The second (Figure 3-11) is concerned primarily with cash flow and maintenance of liquidity. This is no small problem for a company which at the time required $216 million in cash for its operations. Here one also finds organizational recognition afforded to the problems of investment portfolio management. For example, at the time the company listed among its assets $1.6 billion in marketable securities. On the cost side, the firm paid interest charges for the year which amounted to nearly $41 million, with long-term debt of more than $545 million.

The third assistant treasurer (Figure 3-12) is involved in the manage-

Figure 3-10
IBM Finance Staff – Assistant Treasurer I

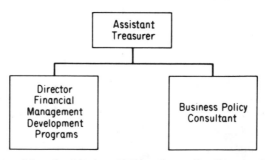

Source: International Business Machines Corporation, November 1966

Figure 3-11
IBM Finance Staff—Assistant Treasurer II.

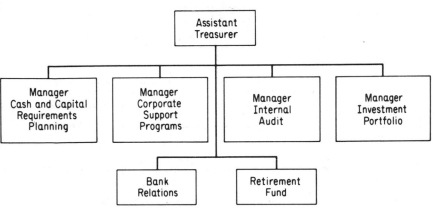

Source: International Business Machines Corporation, November 1966

ment of two major claims on income for a company this size: taxes and insurance. This is no small profit-and-loss item. In 1968, for example, IBM paid federal income taxes amounting to $993 million.

IBM's controller (Figure 3-13) is primarily concerned with corporate control, accountability and measurement. Out of the company's diverse and far-flung efforts must come financial results reported on a consolidated, worldwide basis. Also, at the time there were some 242,000 employees to be paid, and detailed accounting was required for nearly $2.5 billion in retained earnings. No small item in accountability and records keeping was the payment of common dividends of $292.6 million to the company's more than 500,000 shareholders.

Figure 3-12
IBM Finance Staff — Assistant Treasurer III.

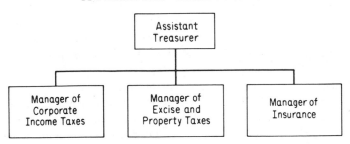

Source: International Business Machines Corporation, November 1966

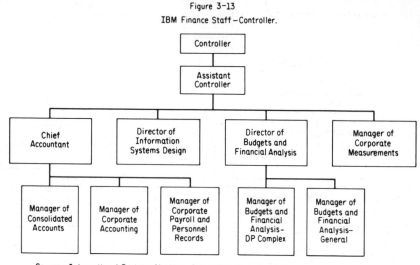

Figure 3-13
IBM Finance Staff – Controller.

Source: International Business Machines Corporation, November 1966

Prudential Insurance Company of America

Finally, let us consider a company with only one-fifth of IBM's employees, but with nearly $28 billion in assets—the Prudential Insurance Company of America. The organization charts of this company give a fairly good idea of the types of functions which are performed by the units depicted.

Since an insurance company is in effect building up claims which it will be called on to honor in the future, often decades later, its key problems are in the area of investment. For Prudential, three of the four departments in the investment area (Figure 3-14) handle major blocks of the company's assets and represent major sources of the company's income. For example, in 1969 Prudential was the holder of approximately $10.9 billion in bonds. An even larger amount of the company's assets was represented by mortgage loans, which amounted to nearly $11 billion. Furthermore, common stock holdings were $2.3 million. The investment area, therefore, constitutes the heart of this firm's operations—in a sense, this is the company's production function.

Managers in the planning and control area (Figure 3-15) work with their counterparts in the investment area to see that this production function is handled in such a manner that the company is assured of perpetual liquidity, and at the lowest possible cost. Furthermore, insurance companies are not entirely free to manage their financial affairs as they please. Reserve

Figure 3-14

Prudential Insurance Company of America—Corporate Home Office, Organization of Investment Area, 1966

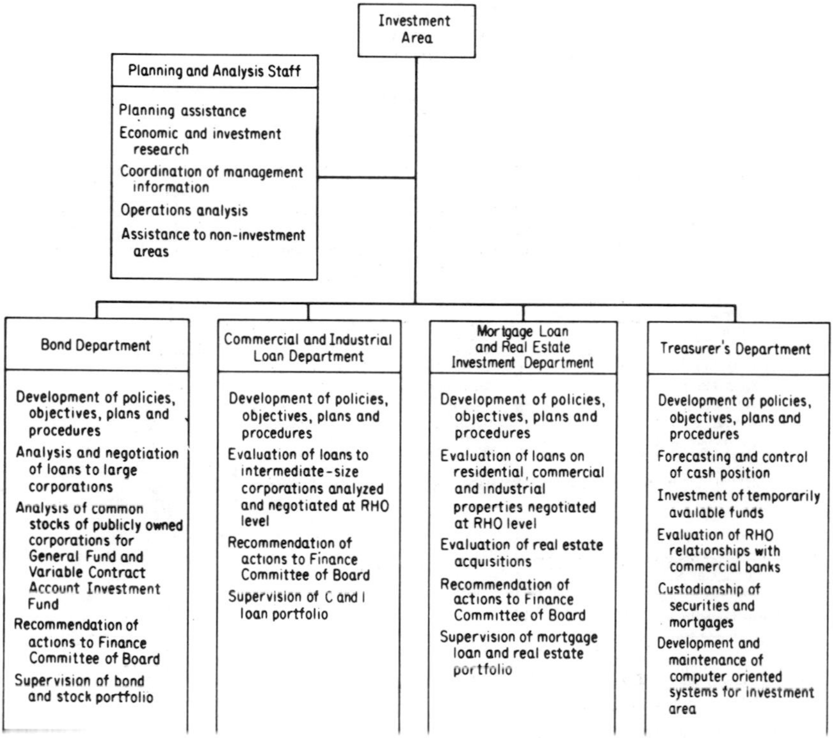

Source: Prudential Insurance Company of America.

requirements and investment practices, which frequently differ by state, are designed to give the policyholder some reasonable degree of assurance that the company will be able to honor its obligations. Careful planning is needed to assure cash flow and liquidity in an enterprise where insurance in force (over $146 billion for Prudential) is more than five times the assets.

Again, Prudential's financial organization reflects the fact that routine handling of receipts and disbursements is no small matter. In 1969 Prudential wrote more than $15 billion in life insurance, received more than $3.8 billion in life insurance premiums, paid out more than $823 million in death benefits and $767 million in policy dividends. A major problem is the fact that field employees (36,051) outnumber home office employees (19,998) by nearly two-to-one, with the former widely dispersed geographically into a great many small, semiautonomous operations.

Figure 3-15

Prudential Insurance Company of America -Corporate Home Office,
Organization of Planning and Control Area

```
                    ┌──────────────┐
                    │   Planning   │
                    │     and      │
                    │ Control Area │
                    └──────────────┘
```

Actuarial Department	Comptroller's Department	Operations Analysis Research Department
For individual coverages: Product development Preparation of forms and rate books Premium rates, earnings and dividends Valuation Actuarial aspects of field compensation Actuarial aspects of insurance services Underwriting policy and manuals Claim policy and manuals For group coverages: Overall review of actuarial and claim matters. Overall guidance on medical matters. Evaluation of RHO actuarial, medical, and claim performance.	Specification of content and maintenance of the books of account for the corporation Preparation and filing of the Annual Statement Administration of taxes Auditing all offices of the Company Establishment of internal controls in connection with all accounting systems	Measurement and evaluation of company performance Information system specification and coordination (including expense analysis) Company long-range and organizational planning Computer equipment planning and research Computer programming research and standards Basic research Planning and Analysis assistance to Area Department.

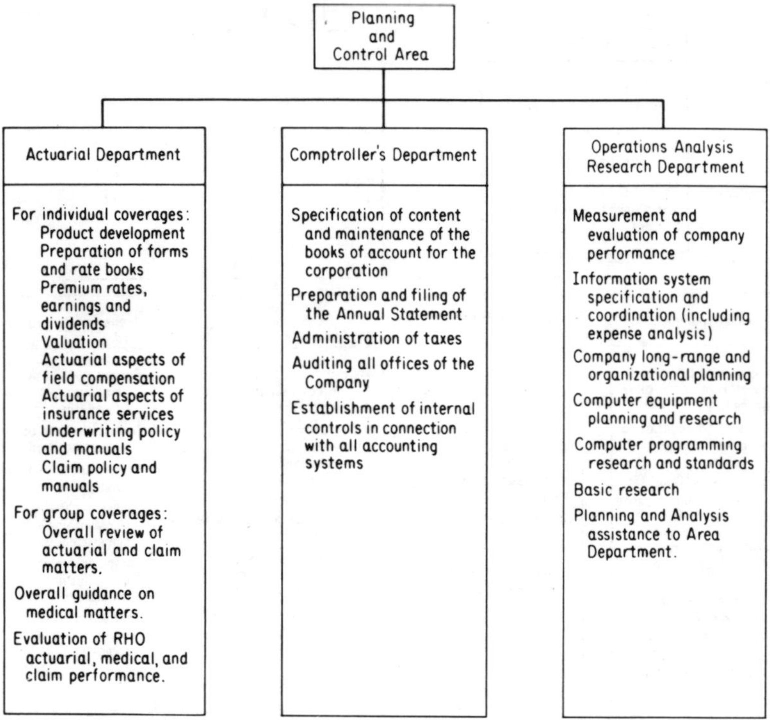

Source: Prudential Insurance Company of America, 1966

SUMMARY AND CONCLUSIONS

Organization charts are merely one way of positioning the employees within a firm so as to facilitate their carrying out corporate objectives. Organization charts define the flow of authority within the firm—that is, they give significance to roles by specifying where the power to authorize or command lies. Frequently they do a very poor job of detailing the flow of information and communications. After all, this is not their primary purpose. Thus the finance, production, and marketing managers may be depicted as being on a common organizational level.

Yet in terms of the extent to which the three functions effectively extend down into the lower echelons of the corporate hierarchy, finance is certainly more pervasive than the other two. One reason for this is the fact that money is one convenient numeraire into which diverse corporate activities may be converted. If activities have a monetary equivalent, they may be controlled by the establishment of standards and budgets in monetary terms. When one accepts the authority of the firm to budget his activities he has implicitly agreed that he will operate only within certain, specified limits. This does not mean that decentralization and fiscal control are inconsistent concepts. Decentralization merely gives the individual freedom in making use of the resources allocated to him.

In this sense, whether finance is a line or staff function is of very little real consequence. The financial manager is vested implicitly with a type of line authority when his budgeting is accepted, and those in the line organization agree to operate subject to a resource constraint. The financial manager operates in a staff capacity when he advises the president and the board as to the consequences of various fiscal alternatives. In his specification and management of the channels which facilitate the flow of financial information he is making the whole concept of a consciously directed, profit-oriented organization a reality.

Since the authority of the financial manager is as much indirect as it is direct, and since he occupies both a line and a staff role in the organization, it is no wonder that organization charts only partly reveal his true significance. Thus analysis of the objectives and techniques of financial management may prove to be a better way of understanding how the finance function is administered than by reference to formal organization charts. This is especially the case in smaller firms, where the formal organization structure is less specified. Indeed, it is often the only practical way of understanding how such firms really operate. For larger firms apparently better organized, job titles can be extremely misleading—to the point that frequently we must go back to the objectives of the organization and analyze how they are in actuality being accomplished. In either case, we are ultimately seeking to get at the *real* rather than the *nominal* basis on which the finance function is being administered.

SUGGESTED REFERENCES

Curtis, Edward T., *Company Organization of the Finance Function*. AMA Research Study 55. New York: American Management Association, 1962.

Firmin, Peter A., and James J. Linn, "Information Systems and Managerial Accounting". *The Accounting Review*, 42 (January 1968), pp. 83–94.

Fox, William M., *The Management Process*. Homewood, Ill.: Richard D. Irwin, Inc., 1963.

Freund, William C., "Seasonal Fluctuations and the Controller's Job." *Financial Executive*, 34 (August 1966), pp. 28–34.

Marting, Elizabeth, and Robert E. Finley (eds.), *The Financial Manager's Job*. New York: American Management Association, 1964.

McGann, T. J., "Controller Belongs on Marketing Team." *Controller*, 29 (August 1961), pp. 377–382.

Plummer, George F., and George Moller, "The Financial Executive." *The Controller*, 30 (January 1962), pp. 16–18, 22, 34–35.

Shubik, Martin, "Objective Functions and Models of Corporate Organization." *Quarterly Journal of Economics*, 75 (August 1961), pp. 345–75.

Weston, J. Fred, "The Finance Function." *Journal of Finance*, 9 (September 1954), pp. 265–282.

4

Investment Decisions I

Riches, like insects, when conceal'd they lie
Wait but for wings, and in their season fly.
—Alexander Pope

Stated generally, the basic questions in finance are these: which assets should the firm hold and which proposed investments should be accepted (and which rejected); and, how should the firm be financed? These are fundamental questions involving both funds sources and funds uses. Since they are stated in normative form, an objective for the firm is assumed. The space limitations of this volume do not permit exhaustive treatment of either issue. Instead, our objective is to identify the problems encountered in making such decisions, and indicate, in general terms, some possible solutions.

INVESTMENT OPPORTUNITIES

In making investments, firms commit funds. Funds are typically looked on as net working capital and more broadly, as anything of value. The funds available to any firm are limited in amount, and all funds have a cost. Because of their cost, these funds should be used in such a way as to attain the objectives important to the firm. Our previous conclusion was that maximization of owners' wealth is the most "rational" objective in a world of uncertainty. Thus we turn to an examination of how financial management seeks to attain this objective through optimal use of the funds available to the firm.

The usual case finds a firm with several alternative projects in which to invest. Each alternative requires an outlay of funds, the amount of which is more or less certain; however, the returns accruing to the firm over time are uncertain. Thus there is a possibility of gain or loss on any given investment. This possibility of loss we define very simply as *risk*. One way of dealing with such a situation is for management to appraise each project on a subjective basis, to assign an expected return (the mean of the subjective probability distribution of possible returns), and to define a measure of the risk associated with receiving the return (usually a function of the dispersion characteristics of the distribution). The above is accomplished on the basis of outcome expectations which are calculated for each project. From this an idea is obtained as to whether any given alternative would tend to increase or decrease the firm's wealth position, and if so, by how much.

Since the funds available to a firm are limited, it is usually the case that all projects likely to increase the firm's wealth position cannot be undertaken. In this event, the financial manager must select those projects that will collectively make the greatest possible contribution to wealth. In doing this, individual investments cannot be viewed in isolation. Each must be seen as an integral part of the firm's composite investments, both existing and proposed.

TRANSACTIONS DEMAND FOR CASH

Before we consider the manner in which funds are invested, let us first consider an important parallel decision which will affect the level of investment, namely, the decison to hold cash balances for transactions purposes. Here one must be concerned with the interesting trade-off between liquidity and profitability. From the overall firm standpoint, cash balances are not usually expected to earn the same rate of return as other investment alternatives, such as investment in assets or distribution to stockholders (who could then exploit higher-valued alternatives open to them). At best, one is probably dealing with the money market rate of return, rather than the much higher rates generally attached to productive investment opportunities. Thus, the financial manager is expected to control cash balances, much in the same way that the production or marketing managers are expected to control inventories.

In exercising this control, it is possible to make use of scientific approaches which, in recent years, have been applied to the management of inventories. The critical issue in inventory management is the estimation of market demand. In the management of cash balances, the key concern is with estimation of liquidity needs. Cash balances provide the liquidity needed to cover the numerous transactions in which a business firm is necessarily involved. Deficiencies in cash can lead to serious operational difficulties and even technical insolvency. It is relatively obvious then that the finance manager must manage for sufficient cash balances; but in the event that he withholds excessive amounts from the purchase of income-generating assets he would violate the wealth-maximization objective considered fundamentally important to normative finance. Rational behavior in the holding of cash balances, therefore, means covering necessary transactions at minimum cost. To abstract from what Keynes termed precautionary and speculative demands, let us consider a simple, hypothetical situation in which transactions are perfectly foreseen and occur in a steady stream.

Assume that a firm has an obligation over a given period to pay out X dollars in a steady stream. To obtain the cash, it must either borrow or withdraw from an investment which in either case would have an interest cost (or interest opportunity cost) of r dollars per dollar per period. Assume also that cash is withdrawn in amounts of Y dollars spaced evenly throughout the year; and each time such a withdrawal is made, a fixed "transaction's fee" of b dollars must be paid to cover imputed and opportunity costs of borrowing or making a cash withdrawal. Thus, X, the value of transactions, is predetermined; and r and b are assumed to be constants. In this hypothetical case, any value of Y less than or equal to X will enable the firm to meet its payments equally well provided withdrawals of the money are made often enough. For example, if X is $1,000, the payments can be met by withdrawing $500 every six months or $250 quarterly or $83.33 monthly, etc. Accordingly, the firm's cash needs will require X/Y withdrawals over the course of the year at a total cost in "transaction's fees" computed by bX/Y.

Routinely then, each time Y dollars are withdrawn, they are spent in a steady stream until they are exhausted; and at precisely that time, a similar amount is withdrawn for steady disbursement, etc. It follows then that average cash balances will be $Y/2$ dollars, and the annual interest cost of holding the cash will be $rY/2$.

The total amount R the hypothetical firm would have to pay for the use of the cash needed to meet its scheduled transactions when it borrows Y dollars at interests evenly spaced throughout the year will then be the sum of interest costs and "transaction's fees" expressed as follows:

$$R = \frac{bX}{Y} + \frac{rY}{2}$$

Since the objective of the financial manager is to cover the transactions at minimum cost, he would accomplish this by choosing the most economical value of Y. One way of doing this is to set the derivative of the above equation for R with respect to Y equal to zero or solve as follows:

$$\frac{-bX}{Y^2} + \frac{r}{2} = 0$$

$$Y = \sqrt{\frac{2bX}{r}}$$

Thus, in the simple example considered here, the rational manager will hold cash balances in proportion to the square root of the value of the transactions to be met.[1] And, in a simplified case, subject to certain assumptions, it is possible to make an optimal decision with respect to the holding of cash balances for transactions purposes. In this we establish a pattern to which we will adhere throughout this book. That is, with a simplified set of assumptions we seek to illustrate that, given the desire to maximize wealth, there are objectively-defensible "solutions" to problems faced by financial managers. Through later discussion, which relaxes some of the simplifying assumptions, we will engage in further development of a decision making model for the financial manager seeking in a systemic context to make funds uses and sources decisions.

In the above case, as the constraints are relaxed, what has been termed the inventory approach to determining optimum cash balances for transactions and other uses becomes more complicated. Each organization that adopts such an approach would probably have built-in peculiarities to incorporate in the cash inventory model. Our intention here has been merely to introduce the concept to the reader, and to develop a line of reasoning which will be used throughout the book.[2]

POSSIBLE USES OF FUNDS

Funds can be used in the following ways. First, assets may be purchased. Second, expenditures may be made for "nonassets" such as research, advertising, interest, personnel development, industrial relations, or legal counsel,

[1]See William J. Baumol, "The Transactions Demand for Cash: An Inventory Theoretic Approach," *Quarterly Journal of Economics,* LXV (November, 1952) pp. 545–556; and James Tobin, "The Interest Elasticity of Transactions Demand for Cash," *Review of Economics and Statistics,* 37 (August, 1956) pp. 241–247.

[2]For further analysis to determine optimum cash balances, see Edward L. Whalen, "An Extension of the Baumol-Tobin Approach to the Transactions Demand for Cash," *Journal of Finance,* 23 (March, 1968) p. 113–134; For management of cash and near-cash assets, see George L. Marrah, "The Corporation and the Money Market," *Financial Executive,* 37 (May, 1969) pp. 83–91.

taking account of the relationship between asset and nonasset expenditures, etc. Third, funds may be distributed to the owners of the firm as dividends or profits. The key role of financial management is to allocate these funds among their various uses in optimal fashion—so as to maximize owner's wealth. In reality, the optimum is probably rarely attained, but this in no way detracts from the value of having this as an objective.

While funds uses have been categorized above as of three possible types, we go on to separately analyze only asset expenditures and dividend distributions (the latter in a later chapter inasmuch as dividend policy cannot be established independently of overall financing considerations). Procedures used to evaluate asset expenditures could readily be applied to nonasset expenditures, therefore, both types of decisions can be analyzed within a common framework. It should be noted that in practice nonasset expenditures are probably subject to much less formal analysis than are asset expenditures if only for the fact that asset expenditures are usually of greater magnitude, or at least represent a larger outlay at a given point in time, or a fixed series of outlays. Furthermore, there is a suggestion that management is subject to a particular type of bias in this respect. For example, far greater attention may be paid to the purchase of a machine costing $10,000 than to an employee who could easily be paid $100,000 during the period of his expected service (and in whom an even larger sum could be invested in training, supervision, or motivation). This may be due at least in part to the fact that asset expenditures are easier to define in terms of the outlays involved, and involve less in the way of hidden, joint, or indirect costs than do nonasset expenditures.

THE INVESTMENT DECISION

In making any investment decision there are several factors to be considered. These may be termed the *basic elements* of the investment decision:

1. Total funds outflows and inflows
2. Cost of funds
3. Timing of the funds flows
4. Risk associated with the funds flow

Most of these elements are difficult to quantify. In fact, differences among various methods for evaluating investment alternatives often reflect different opinions as to the extent to which it is possible to quantify the basic elements of the investment decision. For any method to be totally acceptable, it must take account of all the factors cited. With this in mind, let us consider four methods commonly used to evaluate investment alternatives.

Four Evaluation Methods

Four methods of evaluating investment proposals that have been used are: payback; average rate of return; net present value; and internal rate of return. They may be illustrated by means of a simple example. A firm is faced with a proposal which would require an immediate outlay of $5,000. Assume "certain" after-tax returns over the life of the project (five years) according to the following schedule:

Period

	0	1	2	3	4	5
Outflows	$5,000	—	—	—	—	—
Inflows	—	$1,100	1,210	1,330	1,460	1,500

Assume also that the cost of funds to the firm is equal to 10 percent. With this information we are prepared to address ourselves to the question of whether or not the firm should undertake the investment.

Payback. The usual criterion for payback evaluation is to determine the payback period and then compare it with some predetermined standard. In the example cited, inflows for the first four years total $5,100, which means that the payback period is slightly less than four years, or 3.9 years to be exact. If management adopts a standard to accept proposals with a payback of four years or less, this one would be chosen. Two major weaknesses are attributed to the payback evaluation. The procedure does not consider the time value of money nor the income generated after the payback period.

Average Rate of Return. In using this method of evaluation, we calculate average return as a percentage of original investment or of average investment, where the average investment is equal to original investment divided by two. In this case, total inflows of $6,600 over five years represent an average annual return of $1,320. Average rate of return then, is as follows: $1,320 ÷ 5,000 = 26.4\%$; or $1,320 ÷ 2,500 = 52.8\%$. The return figure selected is then evaluated against some accept-reject standard, as in the case with payback. Typically, this standard is not rigorously defined, and (except by accident) would not be a figure comparable to the cost of capital, nor would it differentiate among levels of perceived or actual risk. The rate of return in this case would be acceptable by almost any standard, and thus if this method is used to evaluate proposals it might very well be undertaken. In fact, a 26.4 percent return is many times the normal after-tax cost of debt. This approach provides misleading conclusions because it contains the same weaknesses as the payback evaluation. To obtain the average rate of return simply divide 100 by 3.9, the previously calculated payback period.

Net Present Value. Another method of evaluating investment proposals requires that all income flows be discounted to the present at an interest rate which reflects the time value of money to the firm (cost of capital). Thus the net present value *NPV* of a proposal is calculated as follows:

$$NPV = \left[\sum_{t=0}^{n} \frac{E_t}{(1+k)^t} \right] - \left[\begin{array}{c} \text{Initial} \\ \text{capital outlay} \end{array} \right]$$

where E is either an inflow ($+$) or an outflow ($-$), t is the period in which E occurs, and k is the cost of funds to the firm.

In the example cited, net present value, assuming a cost of capital rate of 10 percent, is

$$NPV =$$

$$\left[\frac{1,100}{(1.10)^1} + \frac{1,210}{(1.10)^2} + \frac{1,330}{(1.10)^3} + \frac{1,460}{(1.10)^4} + \frac{1,500}{(1.10)^5} \right] - \left[\frac{5,000}{(1.10)^0} \right]$$

$$= \left[1,000 + 1,000 + 1,000 + 1,000 + 932 \right] - \left[5,000 \right]$$

$$= -\$68$$

Since the net present value of this project is less than zero, it would be rejected, because only proposals with positive net present values would qualify for acceptance or be considered likely to add to the firm's value.

Internal Rate of Return. Investment proposals may also be evaluated on the basis of their internal rate of return. The internal rate of return (*IRR*) of a project is that rate which, if used as a discount factor, would make the discounted value of the expected inflows of funds equal to the discounted value of the expected outflows. In other words, the internal rate of return indicates the rate at which cash flows released by the project must be reinvested during the life of the project so as to recover its cost. If this rate is greater than the cost of capital, this means that the funds committed will earn more than their cost. When the *IRR* equals the cost of capital, the firm in theory would be indifferent with respect to the proposal in question as it would not be expected to change the firm's value.

To compute the *IRR* of the project we use the same equation as is used for computing present value. We then set the required outlay ($5,000) equal to the expected stream of income, and solve the equation for the rate r ($r =$ *IRR*) which will equate the discounted value of the expected income stream with the initially required cash outlay. In the example cited r (or *IRR*) is

$$5,000 = \frac{1,100}{(1+r)^1} + \frac{1,210}{(1+r)^2} + \frac{1,330}{(1+r)^3} + \frac{1,460}{(1+r)^4} + \frac{1,500}{(1+r)^5}$$

$$r = 9.7\%$$

This means that a 9.7 percent discount rate would equalize inflows and outflows. This rate is less than the assumed cost of funds (10 percent), and therefore the firm would *not* accept the proposal.

Evaluation of Asset-Investment Proposals

In the analysis above, the payback and average rate of return methods result in a decision to accept the proposal, while the net present value and internal rate of return methods lead to a conclusion to reject it. Which method is "correct"? To shed some light on this question, let us see how the four methods deal with the basic elements of the investment decision.

1. *Funds flows:* All methods recognize that the *amount* of funds required for the proposal is an important factor, but only the last three account explicitly for all funds inflows.
2. *Cost of funds:* The first two methods make no specific allowance for the fact that funds have a cost. The latter two methods, however, treat the cost of funds as an integral consideration.
3. *Timing of funds flows:* All of the methods recognize that returns from the investment will be realized in the future but differ in the way they evaluate expected future returns. Under the payback method the concern is to recover the original investment as soon as

possible. Average rate of return suggests that the average annual productivity of the investment, regardless of when returns are received, is the important consideration. The latter two methods, on the other hand, are very specific in the manner in which they account for future returns by reducing geometrically the value of each dollar received in subsequent time periods.

4. *Risk associated with funds flows:* We assumed in our simple example that returns were "certain or riskless." This is obviously unrealistic. Relax this assumption and none of the four methods yields an "answer." No longer can future returns be projected in any simple fashion—we are now getting close to reality. The financial manager's reaction to such a situation will affect, to some extent, his preference for one method of investment evaluation over another. Either he does the best job he can in subjectively evaluating alternatives and the likelihood of their realization, or he focuses on those projects and methods of evaluation which lead to a preference for early payback. Thus the ability to quantify uncertainty is critical if net present value and internal rate of return are to be used effectively in the world of uncertainty.

It follows then, as we stipulated earlier, that the present-value and internal-rate-of-return methods are the only methods of those listed which give theoretically correct consideration to all elements of the investment decision. Yet the other methods continue to affect the investment decisions made by many firms, probably because they are relatively simple to apply and are familiar through use. Furthermore, businessmen who use these methods often do so because of specific dissatisfaction with the theoretically more defensible methods. Frequently this reflects a concern with the increasing degree to which forecasts are subject to error as the planning period is lengthened. This leads to a preference for projects whose inflows are relatively more certain—a favoring of early paybacks. Furthermore, projects with shorter payback periods may have a greater positive influence on near-term earnings per share, *ceteris paribus*, than those with longer payback periods. If reported earnings are important to the firm, this is not an entirely inappropriate way of evaluating investment proposals.

MAKING THE INVESTMENT DECISION

Let us consider the making of an investment decision starting with one of the theoretically defensible models—internal rate of return—and show

how the basic model that we have used above must be amended if an eco-
nomically optimal decision is to be made.

The Basic Model

If the internal rates of return on several proposed investments assumed
to be equal in risk are computed, we can produce a graph (Figure 4-1)
showing those rates of return that the firm's management expects to earn
on varying levels of dollar investments. It is unlikely in practice that all
these proposals would be relatively homogeneous with respect to risk. But let
us accept this premise for the time being and treat the handling of different
levels of risk only after we have developed a general model.

Theoretically, the investment schedule faced by a firm might take on
almost any shape. Schedules *a* and *b* are merely illustrative of two possibilities, with *a* clearly the more favorable. For example, in the face of schedule *b*,
the firm could invest a total of X_1 dollars with the expectation of earning 20
percent or more. Schedule *a* indicates that a larger amount, X_2 could be invested, again with the expectation being that no less than 18 percent would
be earned on any single investment.

For any firm, given a schedule of its expected rates of return is it possible to determine the level of investment that the firm *should* make by

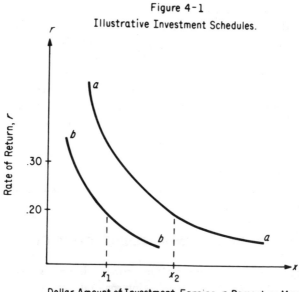

Figure 4-1
Illustrative Investment Schedules.

Dollar Amount of Investment Earning *r* Percent or More

simply taking the amount of funds available for investment, moving out just that far on the horizontal axis, and accepting all the proposals so indicated? It might work out all right, but the weakness is that this approach does not take into account the cost of funds, and hence it may lead to the acceptance of proposals which, if considered in relation to the cost of capital, could not be expected to add to the firm's value.

The Basic Model Amended for Decision-Making Purposes

We must then go one step further if our objective is to determine, given the firm's investment schedule, what the level of investment should be, and which asset proposals *should* be accepted and which *should* be rejected. An equally important question, How should these proposals be financed? will be discussed in a later chapter.

All funds used by the firm have a cost, and will not be used unless the expected return is likely to cover expected costs. For any amount of funds it is possible to compute a schedule of costs, both average and marginal. An illustrative set of schedules is depicted in Figure 4-2. Here we see what happens to the average and marginal cost of funds as the amount of funds needed increases. The average cost of capital schedule depicts the relationship between the amount of financing per period and the dollar-cost per unit of

Figure 4 2

Average and Marginal Cost of Capital Schedules.

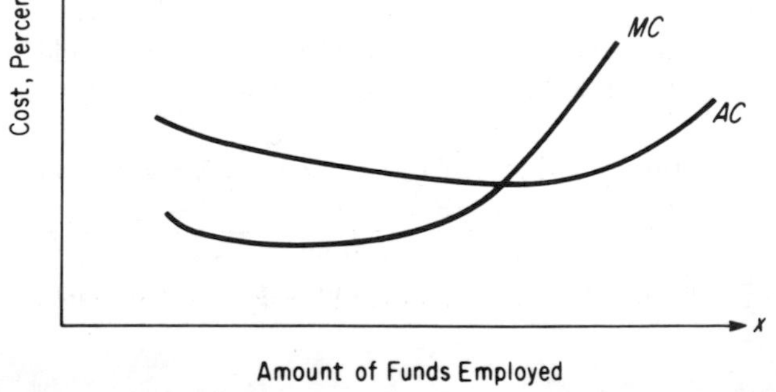

Amount of Funds Employed

financing. As the amount of funds changes, this will most likely change the sources from which funds are obtained, and change the composition of debt and equity. Management's interest in these schedules stems from a desire to discover the most advantageous combination of funds sources—that combination which will supply the requisite funds at the lowest cost.

Given either total, average, or marginal costs, it is possible to compute the others as they are functionally related in a specific way. For example, total cost is the price paid for all funds that the firm employs. Marginal cost measures the rate of change in total cost as one more unit is added, and average cost per unit (e.g., per dollar) equals total cost divided by the unit amounts employed. It must be true that when average costs are rising, marginal costs must be above average costs; if average costs are constant, marginal costs must equal average costs; and if average costs are falling, marginal costs must be less than average costs—although, be sure to note, this does not mean that marginal costs must be falling. Why? Because the price of funds (or their costs) to a firm changes over time, we cannot state categorically that average and marginal costs will rise, fall, or be level as additional funds are raised.

By combining for a firm, an industry, a sector, a country or any other meaningful group, the schedules of funds costs and investment returns, we can visualize how the investment decision can be made (see Figure 4-3).

In this case the marginal return on investment schedule depicting MR assumes that all of the included proposals are equal in risk. This means that the mean value of return expectations may be used in computing internal rate of return or present value. This in turn permits valid comparisons among competing proposals, since all are equivalent in risk.

The intersection of the marginal cost of funds schedule and the marginal return on investment schedule determines how much should be invested, and which investment proposals should be accepted. All proposals with expected internal rates of return down to and including r_x should be accepted, with X_1 being the amount invested in the period. All such projects either add to the value of the firm, or at worst, leave it unchanged. Further, r_x, the rate used to determine whether a specific proposal is acceptable, is also the relevant cost of the funds expended. Therefore r_x is the rate that should be used to discount each project's expected cash flows to determine the project's net present value.

The model stipulates that the total amount invested is determined by the intersection of the MC and MR schedules and that the minimal acceptable rate of return is the firm's cost of funds, or cost of capital. Since the cost of capital is the rate used to discount expected cash-income flows to

Figure 4-3

The Investment Decision Illustrated.

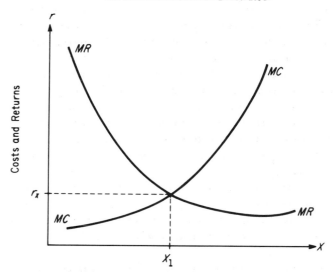

Dollar Amount of Investments, X_1, Yielding r_x Percent or more,
is above intersection of *MR* and *MC*.

the firm, it can be seen that the cost of capital and the value of the firm are
inversely related. Therefore management will attempt to minimize the cost
of capital for any investment level. To the extent that the cost of capital is
a function of the capital structure, management should use that combination of debt and equity resulting in the lowest possible cost of funds. We
must be careful, however, to use this concept correctly as the firm's cost of
capital is basically a function of business risk. Therefore, if a particular
combination of debt and equity leads to a decision to hold a different set of
assets, and if this change in assets leads to an increase in business risk, the
process may, in turn, lead to an increase in the cost of capital. The firm
would then be in disequilibrium, with a change to some other capital structure designed to minimize the cost of capital for the set of assets now indicated. This highlights a real problem in making decisions as to funds sources:
that the type of assets acquired influences the cost of capital and capital
structure and at the same time, the cost of capital and capital structure may
influence the types of assets acquired. Something more is involved, therefore,
than moving to a simple equilibrium position. In practice, an iterative, experimental approach to this problem is not uncommonly taken.

SUMMARY AND CONCLUSIONS

Investment decisions commit funds, which have a cost, to the attainment of objectives important to the firm. Rational financial management seeks to attain this objective through optimal use of available funds.

The typical case finds the firm with a number of projects potentially capable of augmenting its wealth position (assumed to be the firm's objective). Under such circumstances, how is a choice made among alternatives? Making a rational decision in this respect requires that an attempt be made to estimate outcomes and the likelihood of their occurrence. Since we must deal in a world of uncertainty, each investment has a large, almost infinite, number of possible outcomes.

In this context the financial manager seeks to exploit those alternatives that provide the greatest return relative to their cost. This he does through a planned manipulation of funds flows, with specific attention being given to the amount of funds, the cost of funds, the timing of funds flows, and the risk incurred in the process.

Formal methods for the evaluation of investment proposals differ in the emphasis they give to each of the four factors cited immediately above. Present value and internal rate of return are the most defensible from a theoretical standpoint. Their strength stems from the consideration they give to all relevant aspects of the investment decision. Yet it cannot be denied that one sometimes encounters major problems in their application. For this and other reasons, there are substantial numbers of businessmen who use payback, average rate of return, and other theoretically less defensible methods of investment evaluation.

In applying the results of formal evaluation, the principal problem is how to deal with the future. Assuming the dispersion of outcomes is known and that proposals are equal in risk permits the development of a normative model which leads to the greatest revenues in relation to cost. As in traditional economics, the model developed has an equilibrium point where we reach a situation of eventually rising costs or diminishing returns. In practice, difficulties in estimation, and certain interdependencies faced in the process, do not allow the firm to proceed directly to the equilibrium point, even in a situation described in terms of homogeneous risk. Despite difficulties in application, the normative model can be defended as indicating the direction decision-making efforts should take. And, what may be concluded in this respect from the atypical situation defined in terms of homogeneous risk is helpful in charting one's path in the far more complex case of nonhomogeneous risk and uncertainty which is generally characteristic of the real world.

SUGGESTED REFERENCES

Anthony, Robert N. (ed.), "Papers on Return on Investment." Division of Case Reproduction and Distribution, Harvard Business School, 1959.

Bierman, Harold, Jr., and Seymour Smidt, *The Capital Budgeting Decision.* 2nd ed., New York: The Macmillan Company, 1966.

Daellenbach, Hans G., and Stephen H. Archer, "The Optimal Bank Liquidity: A Multi-Period Stochastic Model," *Journal of Financial and Quantitative Analysis,* IV (September, 1969), pp. 329–343.

—"Liquidity Preference as Behavior Toward Risk," *Review of Economic Studies,* 25 (February, 1958), pp. 65–86.

Dean, Joel, "Measuring the Productivity of Capital," *Harvard Business Review,* 32 (January–February 1954), pp. 120–130.

Meyer, John R., and Edwin Kuh, *The Investment Decision: An Empirical Study.* Harvard Economic Studies. Cambridge, Mass.: Harvard University Press, 1957.

Miller, Merton H., and Daniel Orr, "A Model of the Demand for Money by Firms," *Quarterly Journal of Economics,* LXXX (August, 1966), pp. 413–435.

Solomon, Ezra (ed.), *The Management of Corporate Capital.* New York: The Free Press, 1959.

Tobin, James, "The Interest Elasticity of Transactions Demand for Cash," *Review of Economics and Statistics,* 37 (August, 1956), pp. 241–247.

Whalen, Edward L., "A Cross-Section Study of Business Demand for Cash," *Journal of Finance,* 20 (September, 1965), pp. 423–443.

(For other readings on investment decisions, see end of Chapter 5.)

5

Investment Decisions II

The ideas which are here expressed so laboriously
are extremely simple and should be obvious.
—John Maynard Keynes

In our discussion of investment decisions to this point we have used the
term *risk*. Risk refers to nothing more complicated than the possibility that
an adverse outcome might result from any given situation. We developed a
simple normative model which considered alternatives of equal risk. In the
process we avoided the issues of how risk could be measured and what to do
when faced with proposals with different degrees of risk.

It is now our intention to come to grips with these issues, to move into
the real world and the investment problems typically faced by financial managers—and further, to show that this is a world of uncertainty rather than
risk. In order to understand the concept of uncertainty, however, let us first
define uncertainty in terms of the opposite situation, certainty. This will lead
to formal definitions of some key terms, and then into the substance of our
argument.

CERTAINTY AND UNCERTAINTY

The development of a universally valid theory is a very difficult task.
In the social sciences, two major problems are encountered. First, there are
usually many variables affecting and/or relating to the dependent variable
under study. These independent variables may, further, be interdependent
in their influence. Second, it is usually impossible to conduct a controlled
experiment in which all but one, or even some, of the independent variables
are held constant. As a result, in economics and business, theories are developed under assumptions which allow the investigator to concentrate on one
or two variables. Conceptually, this is akin to the manner in which the physical scientist uses repeated, controlled experiments to isolate the effects of one
variable on another.

In this vein let us examine two models of the firm. Both look on profitability as the objective of the firm's behavior.[1] The first model, the *certainty model*, makes this objective clearly definable and attainable. However, this is not the case with the second model—the *uncertainty model*. To illustrate this point, let us first set forth the certainty model and then examine the effect of relaxing some of its basic assumptions.

The Certainty Model

The certainty model assumes the following:

A State of Certainty. The outcome of an event is known and certain—the probability of a specified occurrence is one and the probability of any other event occurring is zero.

Perfect Knowledge. All investors have available the same information at the same time, and at no cost.

Rational Behavior. Investors act rationally on the basis of data provided them. It is assumed that an investor will not accept an inferior or less profitable investment when given a choice. This is a natural consequence of perfect knowledge and risk aversion.

A Perfect Money Market. All investors can borrow or lend all they want at the going rate of interest which remains unaffected by their actions.

No Taxes. There are no taxes.

Costless Transactions. There is no cost for consummating any buy or sell transactions.

Risk Aversion Among Investors. Investors are looked on as being averse to risk. A risk averter, when given a choice between two alternatives, both of which (to him) have the same expected return, but which (to him) appear to differ in risk, will accept that proposal with the least perceived risk. Furthermore, when given the choice between two proposals perceived as having the same risk, but different *expected* values, he will choose that proposal with the highest expected value. Of course, in a world of certainty, risk aversion would not be relevant as the outcome of any investment would be certain and thus risk differences, as well as risk, would disappear.

These assumptions lead to the following model of investment behavior:

---

[1]In the course of the analysis we shall examine the conditions under which such models lead in the direction of our previously assumed objective of wealth maximization.

a firm (as an investor) will accept any proposals with an internal rate of return greater than, or equal to, the cost of its capital inputs. Conversely, the firm would not accept any proposals with a rate of return less than the cost of the capital inputs. The firm would be indifferent about those investments promising a rate of return equal to the cost of the capital inputs, since such investments would not change the net present value of the firm: that is, they would not create an increase in wealth. This is true because any investment whose internal rate of return was equal to the rate at which these returns are discounted, would recoup, or earn, for the firm an amount whose discounted value was exactly equal to the value on a discounted basis of the outlay required to obtain that stream of return. Prove this yourself by reference to an investment analysis in which the rate of return does exactly equal the cost of capital.

To illustrate such a world, assume that the *only* investments available are perpetual bonds, and in this utopian world all bonds of all issuers are riskless. Assume further that the riskless rate of interest is 6 percent. No issuer could sell bonds at a rate less than 6 percent as no investor (knowledgeable, rational, etc.) would invest at, say 5 percent, when his own money cost 6 percent and when other riskless investments yielded 6 percent. *If* for some reason bonds yielding 7 percent became available, they would be purchased immediately and, since they too are riskless, and all investors know about them, the net result will be that the price of these bonds will be pushed up to the point where they too yield 6 percent. Remember that bond prices and interest rates move inversely to one another.

A world of certainty means that profit-maximizing courses of action lead to wealth maximization. Since all investments are riskless, their income streams are all discounted (capitalized in the perpetual case) at the same rate. As a result, any positive addition to profits will result in a positive addition to wealth.

The Uncertainty Model

Once we introduce uncertainty, the simple model which satisfactorily explained investment behavior in terms of profit maximization is no longer adequate. Business firms do, however, operate in an uncertain world. An operationally useful model of firm behavior must take account of this fact.

Some Definitions

First, some definitions are necessary.

Objectively Defined Risk. Objectively defined risk requires that the probability distribution of all expected outcomes be known and objectively determinable (for example, results from tossing a "fair" coin or die). Under such circumstances, risk is commonly expressed as the variance around the objectively determined mean value. This assumes that departures from the mean are *normally distributed*—that is, are random and tend to cancel out. Since it is possible to have two or more distributions with the same means, but different variance, it is possible to obtain varying levels of objectively defined risk.

Uncertainty. Uncertainty is a state of nature which arises when outcomes are unknown and indeterminate. Thus the probability distribution of expected outcomes is unknown or meaningless. Further, there is no mean value and no expected variance around that mean value to serve as a measure of risk. Uncertainty is a subjective phenomenon: no two decision makers will view an event and necessarily formulate the same quantitative opinion. This is because under conditions of uncertainty managers must make choices in an environment of incomplete knowledge.

Subjectively Defined Risk. One way of dealing with uncertainty is to subjectively assign probabilities to estimated outcomes. Through the process, a subjective probability distribution of outcomes is defined.

The above definitions help make precise the types of situations businessmen face. But it is not apparent from them how businessmen react, or should react, when faced with uncertainty. Our primary focus in this book is on the making of decisions. In this respect, let us develop a further concept in quite some detail—the idea of a certainty-equivalent.

Certainty-Equivalents

One way executives can deal with the problems of uncertainty is by thinking in terms of certainty-equivalents. In situations where the outcome is uncertain, the anticipated or expected return—for example, the mean value of all expected returns—on an investment for any given year cannot be expressed in an entirely meaningful way as a single estimate. This will hold true even if this estimate is a best estimate, such as a "most likely" value. For example, assume an investor is offered a choice of a *certain* $100, or a 50–50 chance of either $50 or $150. If his marginal utility of money is constant, then he will be indifferent between the two alternatives. The possible utility gain, U_1, exactly offsets the equally possible utility loss, U_2 (Figure 5-1). If, however, he has a decreasing marginal utility of money, he will then prefer the certain $100. In that event, the possible expected utility loss, U_2, is greater than the equally possible expected utility gain, U_1 (Figure 5-2).

Figure 5-1

Total Utility Curve — marginal utility of money constant

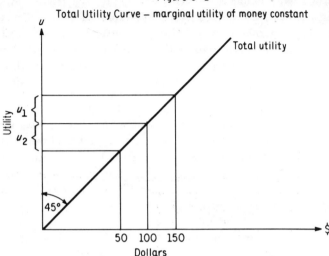

Let us now define a *certainty-equivalent* as that amount of money which an investor would be indifferent to receiving if it were offered as an alternative to an expected but certain amount, E_n, from the investment under consideration. In terms of utility, the gamble represented by the certainty-equivalent is the one that—in this case for the risk averter—matches utility losses and gains. Note that when an investor's marginal utility of money is decreasing, the certainty-equivalent is always less than the expected value.

Figure 5-2

Total Utility Curve — Marginal Utility of Money Decreasing.

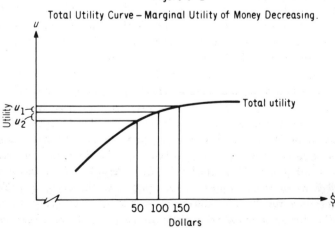

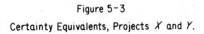

Figure 5-3

Certainty Equivalents, Projects *X* and *Y*.

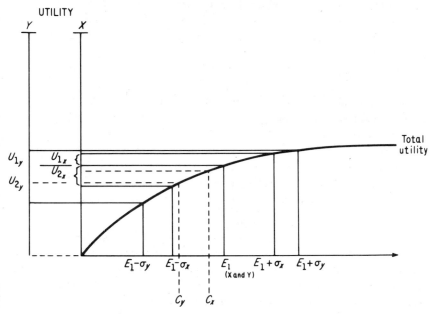

Expected values and certainty-equivalents

Let us advance one more proposition related to certainty-equivalents: the larger the variance around an expected value (E_n), the smaller the certainty-equivalent given the same marginal utility curve. This states, in effect, that as variance increases, subjectively defined risk also increases. Note that this must be so as the variance of the subjectively determined probability distribution is the investor's measure of risk.

In Figure 5-3, assume that project X has an expected value of E_1 and a standard deviation of σ_x and that the possible outcomes are normally distributed. Then $(E_1 + \sigma_x)$ and $(E_1 - \sigma_x)$ have an equal chance of occurring. In order to accept this proposal, the investor would pay up to C_x. Further, suppose that project Y *also* has an expected value of E_1, but has a standard deviation of σ_y, where $\sigma_y > \sigma_x$. Then, for this investor, the certainty-equivalent for project Y would be C_y. C_y is less than C_x even though the expected value of the two proposals is equal since the variance (risk) of X is smaller than for Y. This difference will cause the certainty-equivalent value of X for an investor with given risk aversion to be larger than that for Y. Therefore, for decision-making purposes, the expected value of any project must be adjusted downward by some function of the standard deviation, i.e., $C_x = E_x - \beta\sigma_x^2$, where β is some positive adjusting constant whose magnitude is a function of the marginal utility of money to the decision maker. This factor β thus is an expression of the decision maker's attitude toward risk.

An interesting parenthetical observation is that when the marginal utility for money is increasing i.e., the investing firm is "speculative," then the certainty-equivalent, under conditions of uncertainty, is *greater* than the expected value of the distribution, and the greater the variance the greater is the certainty-equivalent of the distribution. This of course has intriguing implications when one thinks of the use of "certainty-equivalents" in the present value formula. The speculative firm favors projects of the "boom-or-bust" variety, and this preference can be reflected, and justified, through the use of certainty-equivalents.

THE INVESTMENT DECISION RECONSIDERED

The question now remains: How does the certainty-equivalent concept facilitate the making of investment decisions in the case where proposals differ with respect to risk? In the previous chapter it was argued that when proposals did not differ with respect to risk, the intersection of the marginal return on investment and marginal cost of funds' curves determined the point to which investments should be carried. With the use of certainty-equivalents it is possible to derive an overall marginal return on investment schedule, since the proposals under consideration can be adjusted for differences in risk, and therefore can be placed on a comparable basis, in a manner consistent with the attitudes toward risk held by the relevant decision maker.

Referring back to the four evaluation methods discussed previously, we can conclude that the internal rate of return and present value methods of analysis are clearly the superior methods for making investment decisions under conditions of both risk and uncertainty. The reasons for their superiority are that both approaches fully account for all costs, all revenues, the timing of all flows, the cost of capital to the firm, and, through the use of certainty-equivalents, account for risk and risk-differences. Furthermore, it can be shown that both methods are conceptually identical and that they will always lead to the same accept-reject decision. The easiest way to appreciate their equivalence with respect to the accept-reject decision is by noting that at the crucial indifference point the internal rate of return on such a project is equal to the cost of capital and under such conditions net present value of the project is equal to zero. Thus, by both tests—internal rate of return equals the cost of capital and net present value equals zero—management can determine that the project under consideration will make no net contribution to the value of the firm or to the wealth of the shareholders.

RANKING INVESTMENT PROPOSALS

As we have seen, either the internal rate of return or the net present value approaches will give the same signal advice with respect to accept-reject decisions. However, we are concerned with more than accept-reject decisions, for in most cases the shortage of one or more factors of production may necessitate accepting only a fraction of those proposals that are potentially profitable.

Ranking by Index of Profitability

One possible solution to this problem is to compute the net present values (*NPV*'s) of all proposals and then accept those with the highest *NPV*'s. But this is unacceptable as adherence to this rule may lead to the acceptance of a proposal with an *NPV* of $1,000 over ten proposals with *NPV*'s of $100 each, where the cost of the former is $100,000, while that of the latter is only $100 each, for a total cost of $1,000. Thus we may spend $100,000 to get an increment in value of only $1,000 (1 percent of cost) while turning down $1,000 worth of proposals with an individual *NPV* of only $100, but whose total value is the same as we would expect to derive from a commitment 100 times as large.

A way to overcome this particular objection is to compute an index of profitability which adjusts for cost relative to benefits. This may be done in either one of two ways.

1. Divide the present value of the inflows by the present value of the outflows. In this case, the ratio for all acceptable proposals would be 1:1, or more; the higher the quotient, the more acceptable the proposal.
2. Divide the *net* present value by the cost. In this case all acceptable proposals would have a quotient of 0 or more, and again those proposals with the higher quotients would be the most acceptable.

Figure 5—4

Index of Profitability

Proposal (1)	Costs (2)	Benefits (3)	Net Present Value (4)	Index of Profitability 3÷2	4÷2
A	100,000	101,000	1,000	1.01	.01
B	100	200	100	2.00	1.00
C	150	200	50	1.34	.34
D	etc.	—	—	—	—
E	etc.	—	—	—	—

Figure 5-4 provides a tabular example of a profitability index. Using the figures in the example above, it should be obvious that an index constructed either way would rank proposals in the same order.

Ranking by index of profitability raises two other questions. Will this approach signal the acceptance of those projects which are in fact superior? Will this approach rank proposals in the same order as if we accepted proposals in decreasing order of their internal rates of return? Let us answer the second question first. Rankings under these two theoretically correct evaluation (accept-reject) methods may differ. The source of this difference is the differing assumptions made as to the rates at which the cash flows during the period are reinvested.[2]

The Ranking Issue

To see how this ranking difference develops, consider two investment alternatives, A and B, both of which cost one hundred dollars, but with lives of one and three years, respectively. Let us assume that the risk category management attaches to each project is identical, and that the present value of the expected inflows is $13.10 for A and $21.73 for B. Ironically, however, the internal rate of return on project A is equal to 30 percent and that on project B is 22.7 percent. Which project is superior? Is there a way to compare them other than on a basis of total present value or on the basis of their internal rates of return? Which project is expected to add most to firm value, and which ranking method will reveal this?

Plotting the present values on a cumulative basis for each project (see Figure 5-5) helps visualize the problem. This permits us to isolate and to evaluate the effect of various assumptions about reinvestment rates on the investment decision.

While there are a large number of assumptions that could be made about

[2]See Leslie P. Anderson and Vergil V. Miller, "Capital Budgeting: A Modified Approach to Capital Allocation," *Management Accounting*, L, (March 1969), pp. 28–32.

Figure 5–5

Cumulative Net Present Values of Two Difference Proposals
with Identical Costs but with Different Life Expectancies

Year	Discount factor for years 0–3	Project A Expected cash flows	Project A PV of cash flows	Project B Expected cash flows	Project B PV of cash flows
0	1.000	−100	−100	−100	−100
1	.870	130	113.10	0	0
2	.756	0	0	0	0
3	.658	0	0	185	121.73
Total net cash flows		30		85	
Present value of net cash flows			13.10		21.73

Note: An initial investment of $100 is assumed for each project, with a salvage value of zero and a cost of capital equal to 15 percent.

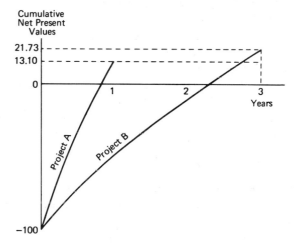

reinvestment rates, historical experience provides evidence which allows the set of possibilities to be delimited. For example, a firm would not expect cash flows from any and all projects to be reinvested at or above the internal rate of return of their "best" investment possibility, nor would they expect the cash flows from any proposal to be reinvested at a rate less than the firm's cost of capital. As a starting point, let us offer two defensible assumptions about the investment proposal: (1) that the funds released by project A can be reinvested at the firm's cost of capital, and (2) that these released funds can be reinvested at project A's internal rate of return. It is obvious that acceptance of the second assumption would result in choosing project A. The assumption that released funds could be reinvested at the firm's cost of capital does not lead to an obvious answer. It must be determined whether reinvestment at the firm's existing cost of capital results in a higher, or lower, net present value for project A when its life is extended to that of the longer-lived proposal, B. Or, what amounts to the same thing, we must determine whether the overall internal rate of return on A is greater than or equal to the internal rate of return on B.

The problem can also be solved for that reinvestment rate, "indifference" rate, which would set the net present values of the two proposals equal at the end of the planning period under consideration, in this case three years. If management were confident that the reinvestment rate on released funds from the shorter-lived proposal would exceed this rate, it would accept A and reject B. The greater the amount by which the expected reinvestment rate exceeded this calculated indifference rate, the greater would be management's assurance in accepting A.

Figure 5-6

Cumulative Net Present Values of Proposals A and B with Different Reinvestment Rates

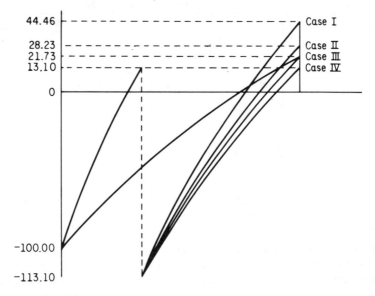

Case I: Reinvestment of cash at proposal A's internal rate of return of .30.

Case II: Reinvestment of cash at the rate of return of project B, .227.

Case III: Reinvestment of cash at the firm's reinvestment at the rate which will equate each project's overall rate of return and its present value.

Case IV: Reinvestment of cash at the firm's cost of capital of .15.

In Figure 5-6 the effect of various reinvestment rates is shown. The following cases are used as illustrations: reinvestment at; (1) 30 percent, project A's internal rate of return; (2) 22.7 percent, project B's internal rate of return; (3) 19.25 percent, a rate such that each project's overall rate of return and present values are the same; and (4) 15 percent, the firm's cost of capital at the time the decision was made.

It should be obvious that there is another aspect to the problem—that a choice of a shorter-lived project always provides management with the opportunity of evaluating the future with the aid of new evidence. It is difficult to assign a precise value to this opportunity, but it would be expected to have a positive value, often a sizable one. While the best that one can do at any given point in time is to act on the basis of the information then available, we do know that more information becomes available with the passage of time. Thus it appears that the value to be assigned to this opportunity to take a fresh look would be a function of, and directly correlated with, the risk involved in the venture: the higher the risk, the higher the value to be placed on the opportunity to reevaluate the proposal.

A Final Note on Rankings

Most managers realize that in order to be able to treat decision problems as mathematical "niceties," they must assign specific values to each element of the relevant equation, even those about which they have serious misgivings. One way to accomplish this is for the decision maker to take these misgivings into account, quantify them, and visualize the results by plotting the Cumulative Present Value (CPV) as a "band."[3] The outer edges of the band or range will represent present values based on the maximum and minimum projected returns and between these outer limits, we could compute the mean expectation.

In conclusion, CPV curves add to an understanding of conventional present worth. It is often stated that while future elements of an income stream are very difficult to estimate, these elements, as time increases, are of practically no importance to the decision maker because they are so heavily discounted. Through the use of CPV it can be seen at just what point in time future returns lose any significant contribution to the present value of a project.

SUMMARY AND CONCLUSIONS

There is little question that *certainty* does not describe the world of business. But, then neither does *uncertainty*. The business world represents

[3]*Ibid.*, p. 30.

something of a mixture of the two. A particular action could lead to a variety of outcomes, since the probability distribution is usually not known and cannot be determined with complete objectivity. But management can determine for most investments the *maximum expected* income, the *maximum possible* loss, and make decisions on the basis of mean expectations between these two limits. What is the basis for estimates of such mean values? It is relevant knowledge of the investment opportunity; its cost; experience with similar investments in the past; expected costs per unit of output; volume of units likely to be sold; expected actions of competitors; costs and prices of competing products; population growth; possible changes in legislation; possible changes in monetary and fiscal policy, etc. Past performance and trends in past performance, present conditions, and predictions about future conditions provide data used by management to estimate possible outcomes and the likelihood of their occurrence. Such data may be the source of a subjectively determined probability distribution of expected returns. The dispersion of expected returns, their mean value, and the shape of the distribution all affect the evaluation of any given proposal.

What is the significance of this subjective, rather than objective, evaluation of alternatives? It means that attempts at profit maximization will no longer necessarily lead to wealth maximization. In the case of decision making under conditions of certainty, choosing the course of action which would maximize profits would also lead to maximization of wealth. Not only are expected returns known with certainty, but the times at which such returns will be received are also known with certainty, and properly valued by an objectively determined discount factor. Such a discount factor, reflecting the premium demanded by a supplier of funds for delaying consumption, is the riskless rate of interest.

In the world of uncertainty, handled through subjective definition of risk, there are two components to the discount factor. The first is the riskless rate of interest; the second is the allowance made for the absorption of risk. This discounting of returns means that they will be reduced because of the allowance made for the risk assigned to the eventuality of their realization. Thus the increment to wealth when risk is present cannot be as large as in the assumed riskless, certain state.

It is interesting to speculate on the nature of the decision-making process in a firm in which the financial manager carries out his job to the ultimate limit of theoretical capabilities. Assume that his weighting of uncertainty represents an accurate quantification of management's utility function. This makes the actual decision trivial. The decision rule becomes: choose the highest-valued expectationally-weighted alternative. This choice could ultimately be safely delegated to a computer. On the other hand, it may be that the ultimate assignment of subjective probabilities to possible outcomes is something that top management either cannot or will not delegate to any lower level. This could be because top management is unable to make precise its attitudes toward the likelihood of undesirable outcomes. But top management may not wish to delegate this responsibility, possibly operating under the theory that this is something that cannot be done at any decision-making level other than the very highest—or that to do so might cause management to fear that they would work themselves out of a job. Whatever the reason, normal business practice defines a role for the financial manager which stops short of the ultimate extent to which his job might be carried with respect to estimation of the risk attached to uncertain situations.

SUGGESTED REFERENCES

Arditti, Fred D., "Risk and the Required Return on Equity," *The Journal of Finance*, 22 (March 1967), pp. 19–37.

Baldwin, R. H., "How to Assess Investment Proposals," *Harvard Business Review*, 37 (May–June 1959), pp. 98–104.

Dickenson, Peter J., "Capital Budgeting—Theory and Practice," *California Management Review*, 5 (Fall 1963), pp. 53–60.

Heebink, David V., and Frederick S. Hillier, "Evaluating Risky Capital Investments," *California Management Review* 8 (Winter 1965), pp. 71–80.

Hertz, David B., "Investment Policies that Pay Off," *Harvard Business Review*, 46 (January–February 1968), pp. 96–108.

———, "Risk Analysis in Capital Investment," *Harvard Business Review*, 42 (January–February 1964), pp. 96–109.

Hillier, Frederick S., "The Derivation of Probabilistic Information for the Evaluation of Risky Investments," *Management Science*, 9 (April 1963), pp. 443–457.

Rappaport, Alfred, "The Discounted Payback Period," *Management Services*, 2 (July-August 1965), pp. 30–36.

Solomon, Ezra, "The Arithmetic of Capital-Budgeting Decisions," *Journal of Business*, 29 (April 1956), pp. 124–129.

6

The Financing Decision

> Money can beget money, and its offspring can
> beget more.—Benjamin Franklin.

We made reference to the cost of funds or capital inputs in the prior chapter on investment decisions and demonstrated that the cost of capital plays a crucial role in the investment decision. In this chapter we address ourselves to the following questions:

What is the cost of capital to a firm? What is its function?

Is there an optimal combination of funds sources which minimizes capital costs?

Is there an optimal timing of funds acquisition?

Collectively, answers to these and closely related questions make up what is termed the *financing decision*. Acceptable answers are hard to derive without some knowledge of money and capital markets, financial institutions, risk and uncertainty, investor psychology, and economics.

THE CONCEPTUAL ISSUE

That funds have a cost should be clear to everyone. In a simple case of borrowing, which involves a contract to repay the amount borrowed plus interest on specified dates, the annual cost is equal to the annual interest paid divided by the amount borrowed. The cost of debt is not always so easy to compute, however, for the reasons that interest may be deducted in advance; there may be a difference between the amount borrowed and the amount to be repaid; interest may be paid quarterly or semiannually. In some cases, currency-value fluctuations may increase or decrease the real cost of debt. In a more subtle and indirect way, current borrowing can make other debt or equity more expensive and these costs must be imputed, or added to, the apparent cost of the debt issue under consideration.

Nevertheless, excluding the problems of imputed costs, the cost of debt is determinable—if not as a precise rate, at least within a relatively small range. In essence, the cost is a function of the net amount of the funds made available, the length of time for which these funds are available, the total amount to be repaid both in the form of interest and principal, and the exact date, or dates, on which these amounts are to be repaid. Given these data we can solve for the rate of interest and internal rate of return that will equate, on a discounted basis, costs and benefits.

It is not as easy to calculate the cost of funds from an equity instrument, because there is neither a stipulated annual or periodic payment (dividends are optional) nor a maturity date or amount. Nevertheless, from the standpoint of the rational purchaser, one would not normally make an ownership investment unless he expected to receive some gain in return; and since, as residual owner, he accepts the greatest risk of any supplier of funds, he will expect a higher return than he would if he were in a more preferred (lower-risk) position.

In order to compute the overall cost of capital inputs to a firm we must take into account the fact that a firm may be financed from a variety of funds' sources ranging all the way from pure debt to pure equity, with hybrids such as preferred and convertible securities in between. In making any and every financing decision, the financial manager must take account of the effect of such financing on anticipated per share earnings, interest and burden coverage, the anticipated multiple at which the stock will sell in the market, and the market yield of the debt.

The effects of each financing decision per se on earnings, and hence on earnings per share and interest and burden coverage, are readily computed when the financing is substitute financing—that is, when the net proceeds of an equity issue are used to retire an equal dollar amount of debt so that there is no net new financing. But it is difficult to predict how the price of the firm's securities will be affected by the change in financial risk. (Note that this business risk has not changed at all—at least not for the moment.) This is so because prices are determined in a somewhat imperfect market made up of rational and irrational investors, risk averters and risk lovers, investors of differing size and with varying levels of influence on prices, and investors with varying degrees of knowledge. Nevertheless, the financial manager, in attempting to minimize the cost of the firm's capital inputs, must deal with the money and capital markets as they exist; and to determine the cost of capital the firm must evaluate all funds sources in terms of their costs. This leads to the question: Is there *a single* cost of capital or *a number* of costs of capital to the firm? To answer this question, extensive analysis is necessarily involved. First, one must consider the sources of capital.

CAPITAL SOURCES AND COSTS

Cost of Equity

It is important to distinguish between the cost of externally raised equity, the sale of securities, and internally retained equity, or retained earnings.

External Equity. The cost of external equity may be expressed in terms of the rate that stockholders demand on an expectational basis in order to induce them to make an equity investment. For the rational investor, that rate is simply the discount rate that an investor applies to expected revenues (dividends *plus* capital appreciation or dividends *minus* capital depreciation) to equate their value with their cost. The relevant discount rate is not one picked at random, but that rate which an informed and rational investor feels he could make on other investments perceived as involving equal risk. The lack of contractually stipulated returns, in the case of equity issues, and the fact that there is neither a maturity date nor amount make this computation difficult. Because of this, investors with the same opportunity costs may develop different opinions about the revenues expected from a given firm's shares, and react differently to given share prices. The same line of reasoning may be used to explain the behavior of owners or short-sellers who make up the supply side. The price of a share of stock at any given point in time is thus determined by decisions and actions based on expectations of the marginal buyer and seller.

It will be noted from the above that the shareholder's investment decision is based on the same criteria as the firm's investment decision: cost and revenues, their timing, risk, and the costs, or returns, perceived to be currently available from other investment opportunities. In any investment decision, whether directly in real assets, or indirectly in securities, the investor must take into account all the relevant considerations capable of affecting its outcome.

One way of calculating the value of any asset is to discount the expected future benefits at the rate deemed appropriate by the investor. The implications of such an approach have been discussed previously. Thus the value of a share of stock may be expressed as follows:

$$V = \frac{D_1}{(1+k)^1} + \frac{D_2}{(1+k)^2} + \cdots + \frac{D_n}{(1+k)^n} + \frac{U_n}{(1+k)^n}$$

where V = value or price per share; D_n = the expected dividend in year n; U_n = the expected price of a share in year n; and k = the investor's required rate of return. If, in the investor's mind, dividends are looked on as perpetual, and equal in each period, one could express share value as $V = D/k$. This is so because given the two assumptions stated for the latter case the formulas are algebraically equivalent.[1]

If, as in the more usual case, the investor expects the firm's earnings to increase over time, and hence to receive continually greater dividends, an adjustment of the valuation formulation is required to take account of this expectation. For simplicity, assume that all investors expect a firm's dividend, D, to grow at the rate g forever. The value of a share would then be[2]

[1] If $D_1 = D_2 = D_3 \cdots = D_n \cdots = D_\infty$, $(= D)$ then the value of the income stream would be

$$V = \frac{D}{(1+k)^1} + \frac{D}{(1+k)^2} + \frac{D}{(1+k)^3} + \cdots + \frac{D}{(1+k)^\infty}$$

$$= \frac{D}{1+k}\left[1 + \left(\frac{1}{1+k}\right) + \left(\frac{1}{1+k}\right)^2 + \cdots + \left(\frac{1}{1+k}\right)^\infty \right]$$

If we let $\frac{1}{1+k} = r$, then the value of the geometric progression $[1 + r + r^2 + \cdots + r^\infty]$ can be shown to be equal to $\frac{1}{1-r}$, and we have

$$V = \frac{D}{1+k}\left[\frac{1}{1-r} \right]$$

$$= \frac{D}{1+k}\left[\frac{1}{1-\left(\frac{1}{1+k}\right)} \right]$$

$$= \frac{D}{1+k}\left[\frac{1+k}{k} \right]$$

$$= \frac{D}{k}$$

[2] Assuming that the firm retains a constant percentage of its earnings and earns on them a constant rate r, where r is greater than k. This is merely a formal way of quantifying what is commonly referred to as a firm's "growth" prospects.

$$V = \frac{D}{(1+k)^1} + \frac{D_1\,(1+g)}{(1+k)^2} + \frac{D_1\,(1+g)^2}{(1+k)^3} + \cdots$$

$$+ \frac{D_1\,(1+g)^{n-1}}{(1+k)^n} + \frac{U_n}{(1+k)^n}$$

Furthermore, the value of any share at any point in time, t_1, or t_n or t_{n+m}, is equal to the discounted present value of dividends expected from that time forward.

Given these assumptions, it is possible to sum the series and, provided k is greater than g, derive a price formula for a share of stock (about which all investors share similar growth expectations) in terms of the firm's currently expected dividend, D_0. This gives us

$$V = \frac{D_0}{k-g}.$$

In words, the value of a share, or its price, is a function of the current dividend, and the difference between the investor's required rate of return and the rate at which these dividends are expected to grow. One would expect that as g grows, k will grow, and an observation of the performance of stock prices would lead us to conclude that the difference between the two will get smaller. That is, that the price per dollar of current dividends, or earnings, will be higher the faster the rate at which investors expect g to grow. To test the validity of this conclusion, examine the price movement of growth stocks, e.g., IBM, Polaroid, Leasco, and others.

Since our concern is in establishing the cost of equity capital k, we restate the formula developed above in terms of k:

$$k = \frac{D_0}{V} + g$$

Thus, given the assumptions inherent in our analysis, the cost of equity capital can be expressed as a function of the current dividend, the current price, and the rate at which investors expect the dividend to grow.

There are alternative measures of the cost of equity capital, but these do not take growth into consideration; we merely mention them in passing. The two other most often cited formulas for computing equity costs are

$$k_e = \frac{E}{P} \quad \text{and} \quad k_e = \frac{D}{P}$$

where k_e = cost of equity capital, E = earnings, D = dividends, and P = price. The former involves a problem in double counting. If one eliminates this, the earnings model reduces to the dividend model. The latter is easily derived from the approach we suggested above where $k_e = \frac{D}{P} + g$. If the expected growth in dividends equaled 0, then the g term would drop out. Thus, $k_e = \frac{D}{P} + g$ is generally useful in almost every situation at the stipulated levels of abstraction with which we are working.

We say in *almost* every situation because this approach is not applicable where the company currently pays no dividend, e.g., in a case such as Litton Industries, and it is not entirely meaningful if the current dividend is an extremely low percentage of earnings, but the payout ratio is expected to change. Furthermore, we have made certain assumptions and to the extent that such assumptions are not realistic, the operational usefulness of the model is adversely affected.

Internal Equity. Retained earnings in common with all capital have a cost, and this amount may be expressed as a percentage of the cost of externally raised equity by evaluating their price on the basis of the stockholders' personal situation. Since dividends paid out are taxed to the holder at his marginal tax rate, the cost of retained earnings may be looked on as equal to the cost of existing equity times 1 minus the relevant investor marginal income tax rate. For example, to be conservative, we assume that investors are subject to at least a tax rate of 20 percent even though the rate may vary widely. To them, this makes the cost of retained earnings equal to $k(1 - .20)$, or $0.8k$.

An exact formulation of the cost of retained funds based on the personal use approach presents formidable difficulties if the assumption of uniform tax rates is lifted. In Ezra Solomon's view, however, it is unnecessary to pursue these refinements. He concludes that the proper measure of the opportunity cost of any course of action, in this case the proposed internal investment, is the best alternative opportunity the course of action forces us to forego, and at minimum this is equal to k_e, the yield available on external investment.[3] In other words, so long as external opportunities are available,

[3]See Ezra Solomon, *The Theory of Financial Management* (New York: Columbia University Press, 1963), pp. 54–55.

the minimum measure for the cost of internal funds is k_e, regardless of the effect of personal taxes.

Cost of Debt

Existing Debt. The cost of debt is equal to that discount rate, or internal rate of return, which would set the present value of future payments, both principal and interest, equal to the net amount received from the issue. If the firm anticipates investor evaluation correctly, it can, should it so desire, successfully sell new bonds at a price that will net, after all underwriting and flotation costs, the face amount of the bond, or par. In that event the coupon rate would equal the investors' required rate of return. If the coupon rate is less than the investors' required rate of return, the bond will sell below par; if above, the bond will sell above par. In any case the cost of debt is that discount rate which equates costs and benefits.

The cost of a debt issue then, sold at par, is approximately equal to the following: $k_d = \dfrac{I}{P_d}$, where k_d = cost of debt, I = interest, and $P_d = MV_d$ = price and maturity value. Both the numerator and the denominator must be adjusted when the bond sells at either a premium or a discount from par, $(P_d \pm \Delta)$. The pro-rata difference between maturity value and current market price (negative for a premium sale; positive for a discount sale) must be added to the numerator, I. The denominator must be adjusted by the average of the bond's current sale price and its maturity value (where $P \neq MV$). Thus in the case of a bond sold at a discount, the cost, k_d, would be approximately equal to the following:[4]

$$k_d = \frac{I \pm \dfrac{\Delta}{n}}{\dfrac{P + MV}{2}}$$

Since interest payments are a tax deductible expense to the firm, the after-tax cost of debt is equal to $k_d(1 - \text{firm's tax rate})$. If firms earning more than \$26,000 per year are taxed at 48 percent of taxable earnings; there-

---

[4]The average amount of capital available to the firm is approximated by arithmetic averaging: $\dfrac{P + MV}{2}$. A precise cost figure could be obtained from a bond table.

fore, their after-tax cost is $k_d(1 - .48)$, or slightly more than one-half the before-tax cost. For firms earning less than $26,000 a year, the marginal tax rate would be 24 percent; therefore, the after-tax cost is $k_d(1 - .24)$, or approximately three-fourths of the before-tax cost.

New Debt. We cannot dispense with the cost of debt as easily as the foregoing suggests. If a firm acquires new debt and uses the net proceeds to retire an equal dollar amount of equity, the transaction results in an addition to the financial risk of the firm. But since the money that was raised was not used to change the assets of the firm, the business risk of the firm probably has not changed. We might conjecture that a less conservative capital structure could very well change management strategy, could change the management itself, and/or could have been brought about by new management. It is easy to see the role and importance of assumptions in financial analysis. Since this additional risk, along with existing business risk and prior financial risk, is borne by the common shareholder, his required rate of return should go up as a consequence. Thus in computing the cost of new debt we must add to the rate of discount required by bondholders an allowance for the imputed cost attached to such debt, i.e., the increased return required by the stockholders.

The magnitude of the premium required by shareholders as compensation for added risk is difficult to determine empirically. Accordingly we do not attempt to adjust k_d in the general formulation. Let us at this introductory level simply recognize that risk to the shareholder is increased when the proportion of debt to equity is increased and that a rational, risk-averting, and knowledgeable shareholder will now require a greater return.

For example, let us assume a firm with 10 percent debt and 90 percent equity, and after-tax costs of $3\frac{1}{2}$ percent and 12 percent respectively. Overall cost may be stated as a weighted average as follows:

Weights Percent		Cost		Totals
.10	$\times$	.035	$=$	.0035
.90	$\times$	.120	$=$	.1080
1.00			$=$	.1115
Weighted average cost			$=$	$\dfrac{.1115}{1}$

Now the question is—could the firm lower its cost of capital, all other things being equal, by selling bonds and using the proceeds to retire common stock? It could, provided the expected increase in the cost of equity would not offset the advantage gained by making greater use of what was originally the lower cost alternative, debt.

Cost of Preferred Stock

While preferred stock is defined legally as an equity issue, it has characteristics of both debt and equity. In the usual case, preferred stock is a fixed-income security with return limited to a stipulated dollar dividend or a percentage of par value, as set forth in the preferred-stock contract. On the other hand, the rights of the preferred stockholder in case of dissolution come after the claims of all creditors, but before those of the common stockholder; and, like common equity, the preferred issue has no maturity date.

The current cost of preferred stock is

$$k_p = \frac{D_p}{P_p}$$

where k_p = cost of preferred stock, D_p = the stipulated preferred stock dividend, and P_p = the current market price. Thus for financial purposes it can be seen that the costs of preferred issues are calculated in the same way as are the costs of debt.

Cost of Leases

Leases, while not a security in the usual sense, are an increasingly important source of funds and, at least for the ongoing firm, the financial contract covering leases differs from a bond contract more in form than in content. A financial lease is one in which the lessee contracts to pay for the entire cost of the asset leased, plus interest charges, to the lessor, over a stipulated period of time. For a firm that raises money in this form let us compute the cost incurred.

As indicated, a lease is roughly equivalent to a debt agreement in that in both cases the borrower (lessee) repays the lender (lessor) the amount borrowed (the value of the assets), plus periodic payments to the lessor to cover interest or financial charges. These charges are related to the risk involved and also to the bargaining power of the parties involved. Thus a lease may be looked on as a special form of borrowing closely resembling those debt agreements that require the serial or periodic repayment of principal in addition to the periodic payment of interest.

The cost of a lease can be approximated by dividing the periodic interest costs by the amount received. As in the case of new borrowing, new leases also have an imputed cost element, namely the cost of the differential rate of return that stockholders and bondholders may now demand since the firm has taken on increased financial risk.

THE OVERALL COST OF CAPITAL

Upon reflection we can see that the opportunity cost principle underlies all decisions to invest. For example, we saw that the price of a share, or a bond—or in fact, of any asset in a free market—is determined by the marginal buyer and seller. And how do these parties to a transaction determine their respective price limits? By establishing the subjective risk attached to the asset in question and comparing it with the risk perceived as being attached to all other assets—assets subject to the same, greater, and lesser levels of perceived risk. If the rate of return that could be earned on other assets of the *same* risk (in the same risk class) was k_r, then the investor would demand at least k_r from the asset under consideration.

When we noted earlier that a buyer (or seller) established the price he was willing to pay by discounting his expected future returns at *a rate* he deemed to be appropriate, we were referring to his "opportunity cost" rate— or the rate that he could earn on "similar" investments. Thus, with respect to any funds available to the firm, we can simply say their cost is equal to the firm's present weighted average cost of capital.

The Weighted Average Cost of Capital

Earlier we made brief reference to the weighted average cost of capital. It is this capital cost that we consider to be the relevant cost of the existing capital to the firm. This cost is derived through reference to the price at which the firm's various securities sell in the market, and then computing the weighted cost of these notes, bonds, preferred and common equities. The cost of retained earnings is then derived from the cost of common equity, and a weighted average cost is computed. We previously concluded that the cost of depreciation, depletion and amortization is equal to the firm's cost of capital. If this is the case, it may be excluded from our computations.

For example, in a hypothetical situation, the cost of capital could be computed as follows:

	Percent of Total	Cost Before Tax	Tax Adjustment	After Tax Cost
Bonds				
First mortgage	.1	.050	1—.48	.025+
General debentures	.1	.060	1—.48	.030+
Subordinated debentures	.1	.066	1—.48	.033+
Preferred stock	.1	.070	None	.070
Common stock	.6	.120	None	.720
Weighted average cost	1.0			.878

Computing the cost of capital to an actual firm in the real world is not so simple, for the following reasons:

(a) Bonds may not be publicly traded and a current price will have to be estimated.

(b) Securities may be traded, but their market prices for one reason or another may not be deemed to reflect a market of any depth and an adjustment may be anticipated.

(c) The rate at which shareholders expect dividends to grow must be estimated.

(d) The shareholder's required rate of return will have to be estimated.

(e) The relevant marginal tax rate of investors will have to be estimated and averaged.

(f) The marginal utility of money to stockholders will have to be estimated and averaged.

Thus in computing the cost of capital inputs to the firm, management may in light of the above think of the cost of capital as falling within a range of values. In turn, when using the cost of capital as a cutoff rate, management will need to take extra care in approving a project whose rate of return approaches what to them is the relevant cost of capital.

OPTIMAL COMBINATION OF FUNDS SOURCES

To determine what the capital structure of the firm *should* be involves definition of that capital structure which minimizes the cost of capital inputs and, therefore, which maximizes the per share value of outstanding stock. What is this capital structure and how is it determined? There are several theories; let us examine them briefly.

The Traditional View[5]

According to this view, the cost of capital to a firm, as a function of its capital structure alone, is looked on as being V- or U-shaped. This means that the cost of the capital inputs is a decreasing function of the amount of debt, up to some point, or set of points.

Graphically, the traditional view is set forth in Figure 6-1.

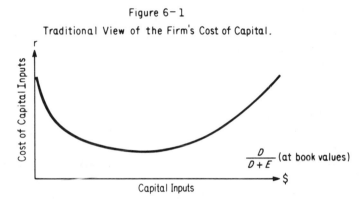

Figure 6-1

Traditional View of the Firm's Cost of Capital.

This view assumes that low-cost debt is successfully substituted for higher-cost equity, up to a point. But little is offered in the way of explanation as to why this should be so, and there are few rigorous attempts to define where the minimum point or range may be located. As a result, vague rules of thumb were developed which both firms and investment bankers tended blindly to follow. As one financial officer put it to one of the authors: "We are advised by our investment banker to keep our ratio of debt to equity at or below 15 percent. But why this level? Because it is the average level of the industry. And why is it the average level of the industry? Because it is our ratio and we are the leading firm in the industry. So therefore we do what the average is, and the average is what it is because that is what we use."

It should be noted in passing that one should not use the above line of reasoning as the sole basis for not setting this and other corporate policies in relation to industry-wide standards. It may be that those firms which sur-

[5]While some label may be better than "traditional," it is used here to refer to the view most often expounded in the textbooks on finance—most usually corporate finance—up to the 1950's. The reader should not confuse this with the so-called "traditional" approach to finance—discussed in Chapter 1. For lack of a better alternative the same descriptive terms are used.

vive in an industry do so because they were the ones who for valid or invalid reasons were able to discover certain viable operational standards. Furthermore, if firms not operating at viable levels failed to survive, then emulation of the behavior of survivors may indeed be a valid operational principle. However, with experience it is assumed that logical explanations and reinforcing empirical data will serve to validate the relevance of operational standards followed on an industry-wide basis.

It is not clear that the traditional view of capital structure has been so validated. There is no lack of academic comment supporting the view, even though the optimal level is not well defined, nor well defended. It is also clear that business firms develop perceptions of their own risk levels and, on the average, the greater the risk, the lower the ratio of debt to equity in their capital structures. Apparently businessmen feel that charges for debt should be adjusted to levels that the firm's cash flows will "safely" support.

The Modigliani-Miller View

A rigorous challenge to the traditional view was supplied by Professors Franco Modigliani and Merton H. Miller.[6] Other important contributors, however, made significant progress in dealing with this issue. (In a real sense much of the contemporary thought in this area stems from the work of David Durand of M.I.T.)[7]

According to this position, and under certain assumed conditions, the cost of the capital inputs to the firm remains unchanged as the result of raising part of the firm's funds through debt. Such a conclusion is based on the assumption that you cannot change the price at which an asset (a given income stream) sells merely by changing the form in which it is sold. Assuming (1) no taxes, (2) perfect capital markets, (3) an investor's ability to borrow against stock pledged as collateral at the same rate that a firm could borrow, and (4) costless transactions, they substantiated their position by demonstrating that two identical income streams could not sell at different prices. If one income stream should sell in the market at a higher price simply because it was either levered or unlevered, investors—regardless of their attitudes toward risk—could improve their return by selling the overpriced shares and buying the underpriced shares. In the process they would introduce as much leverage in their personal account as the firm had in its

---

[6]Franco Modigliani and M. H. Miller, "The Cost of Capital, Corporation Finance, and the Theory of Investment," *American Economic Review*, XLVIII (June 1958), pp. 261–297.

[7]David Durand, "The Cost of Debt and Equity Funds for Business: Trends, Problems of Measurement" in *Conference on Research in Business Finance* (New York: National Bureau of Economic Research, 1952).

Figure 6 - 2

Hypothetical Market Valuation of Two Firms,
Identical in All Respects,
Except That of Financial Composition
(In a World of No Taxes)

	Two Identical Firms Except for Financial Structure	
	A	B
Income	1,000	1,000
Debt	0	4,000
Interest rate.....................	—	.08
Annual interest	0	320
Income after interest..............	1,000	680
Payout ratio (dividends as percent of income after interest)	100%	100%
Capitalization rate on after interest income	.10	—
Value of equity (assumed market valuation)	10,000	7,000
Total value	10,000	11,000

account, and thus the risk exposure of the investor would not change. They called this trading transaction *homemade leverage*. An example is shown in Figure 6-2.

In the table of Figure 6-2 it is hypothesized that a firm can change the price at which it sells in the market by changing the form in which it is financed. If this is possible, then we are able to prove that the cost of capital to a firm is U- or V-shaped or at least that it is a decreasing function of the amount of debt, up to some point.

Examine the following: Assume that an investor owned 10 percent of B's, the overvalued firm's equity from which the investor would receive $100 income. As a rational investor, with complete knowledge, he recognizes that the riskiness of the income streams of the two firms, before interest requirements, is equivalent; further, as a rational, risk-averting investor he wants to know if he can improve his return without changing his exposure to risk. Let's see.

Suppose he sells his stock in Company B for $700. He then uses the proceeds to buy $700 worth of stock in Company A and, further, pledges the new stock as collateral for a loan of $400 in order to buy additional stock in Company A. He has thus introduced the same leverage in his personal account as existed in the corporate account: $4 of debt for every $7 of equity.

The net result is that the investor now owns 11 percent of the under-valued firm, from which he receives dividends of $110. But he must pay 8 percent interest on his debt of $400, or interest of $32. His new invest-ment thus provides him with $78 after interest as compared with $68 he obtained on his prior (original) investment. Without changing his risk ex-posure because he has introduced as much risk in his personal account as existed in the corporate account, he has improved his return.

Modigliani and Miller posit that this switching will continue until both income streams sell in the market for the same price. Given no taxes, they conclude that the cost of capital to a firm is equal to the capitalization rate of a pure equity stream and that the rate, or cost, is a constant and not func-tionally related to the amount of debt used by the firm.

Introduction of taxes changes the picture substantially. There is a differ-ential tax treatment to the firm of interest and dividends, with the former being a tax-deductible expense. To the individual investor there is also a difference, albeit on the average quite small, due to the fact that the first $50 of dividends received per individual in any tax year is tax-free. However, we disregard `the latter difference, which if at all measurable, is measurable through its influence in the demand for stocks, shifting the demand curve to the right.

We will now concentrate on the effect of the tax-deductibility of inter-est payments to the firm. Removing the assumption of no taxes, in order to correspond to reality, leads to a modification in the conclusion. The introduc-tion of taxes on income after interest, means that the levered firm B would pay less taxes and therefore that the net cash flow available to the firm after taxes, for interest, dividends, or reinvestment is greater for the levered than for the unlevered firm. This leads to the conclusion that the cost of capital to a firm is a steadily (linearly) decreasing function of the amount of debt. Graphically portrayed, the resultant schedule of the cost of capital as a func-tion of increasing leverage is as shown in Figure 6-3.

On the surface, this leads to the conclusion that an optimal capital struc-ture would be almost 100 percent debt. But in practice, this sort of capital structure is nonexistent. It must be then that either the theory is invalid or that firms are not managed in an optimal manner. To bring this statement into proper perspective, let us see if we can find explanations of why firms have set limits on debt and examine the reasonableness of these limits.

Corporate Debt Capacity

As noted earlier, the fixed cash costs of debt have, at times, been fatal to a firm or to certain classes of securities holders. Thus, even though there may be a cost advantage to debt, debt has been limited in amount.

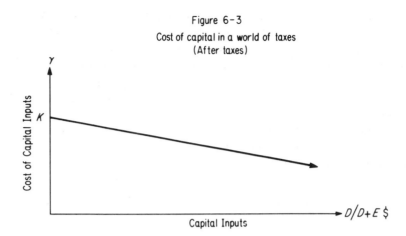

Figure 6-3

Cost of capital in a world of taxes
(After taxes)

Professor Gordon Donaldson has analyzed the question of debt levels by asking the following question:[8] How much debt or fixed financial charges can a firm carry and still maintain, with required assurance, some minimum interest and burden coverage below which they are not likely to fall? In most cases this minimum would be approached during a period of recession or depression. Therefore his suggestion is that a firm develop a recession cash-flow analysis and use as a top limit that amount of debt that the firm could carry under these conditions.

A combination of the Donaldson and the Modigliani and Miller analyses leads one to take this position: Due to the tax-deductibility of interest, debt has a cost advantage to the firm. But there are limits to the extent to which the firm can take advantage of debt. One limit would be that amount of fixed financial charges the firm could carry under the worst conditions felt "likely" to occur. Here, as was true in the investment decision, the importance of individuals must be stressed. One management group may tend to be pessimistic while another may be more optimistic about the future. As a result, if both managements were to use debt to the maximum limit possible, the optimistic management would use more debt. Further, one would expect that the investment decisions of the two firms would be quite different.

Debt limits may also come from the market. At any point in time, a firm would find a limit to the amount of debt it could sell at rate X—a limit to the amount it could sell at rate $X + \Delta X$, etc. The increased cost would be the reflection of the increased possibility of loss, and successive bond issues of the firm might fall into lower and lower ratings as the firm pushed its

[8]Gordon Donaldson, *Corporate Debt Capacity* (Cambridge: Harvard University, Graduate School of Business Administration, Division of Research, 1962).

use of debt. If management wished to be relatively sure that its bonds would continue to be rated at some level or above, e.g., AA or A, it may set limits on the amount of debt incurred. Thus corporate prestige or other behavioral factors may affect the use of debt, with, for example, the relevant consideration being the prestige of having bonds rated at a certain level or above. Could a money value be set on this prestige rating? And, if so, could not the management then evaluate the alternatives? Further, boards of directors are often made up of bankers and investment bankers, and these men, if they are conservative, tend to establish conservative policies with respect to the acquisition of debt.

SUMMARY AND CONCLUSIONS

In this chapter we have examined the financing decision in light of the firm's cost of capital. Upon reflection, it turns out that there is no single cost of capital to a firm, but a weighted average cost which considers all capital sources and the extent to which they are used. In the real world there are several sets of conditions that can make this weighted average cost difficult, if not impossible, to compute.

The second major issue considered is the extent to which a firm is able to develop some optimal combination of funds sources or capital structure. The traditional view that the cost of capital inputs is a decreasing function of the amount of debt up to "some point," after which the cost will then rise, is given considerable attention. The work of Modigliani, Miller, Donaldson, and others is used to bring the issue into its proper perspective.

This leads to the conclusion that acceptable debt limits for a firm can probably be defined within a certain range, and that these limits are a function of both firm variables and market variables. But an observation of firm and market behavior does not indicate that there is a continuous advantage to the use of debt. Is this true?

We cannot answer this question with assurance. There are not presently available empirically derived measures of capital costs in relation to leverage—studies sufficiently free from bias to be considered conclusive.

Thus we take the following position on capital structure. Given certain rather artificial assumptions, one could well argue that the cost of capital inputs is a decreasing function of the amount of debt in the capital structure, and that this cost advantage is derived from the tax deductibility of the interest payments. But in a world of imperfect capital markets, imperfect knowledge, particular attitudes toward the riskiness of debt, and an inability in most cases for investors to divide firms into narrowly defined risk classes, the evidence seems to suggest that the cost of capital is a U- or V-shaped function, as posited by the traditional writers.

It has been the purpose of this chapter to identify this important problem and to point out how the problem can be analyzed. A conclusive answer to the general question of how a firm should be financed, and exactly what its capital structure should be, may not be possible in the real world. But, improved statistical analysis, using such approaches as factor and cross-section analysis, may provide a more nearly definitive solution.

SUGGESTED REFERENCES

Archer, Stephen H., and LeRoy G. Faerber, "Firm Size and the Cost of Externally Secured Equity Capital," *Journal of Finance*, 21 (March 1966), pp. 69–83.

Gordon, Myron J., and Eli Shapiro, "Capital Equipment Analysis: The Required Rate of Profit," *Management Science* 3 (October 1956), pp. 102–110.

Jeynes, Paul H., "Evaluating the Cost of Capital," *Financial Analysts Journal*, 20 (July–August 1964), pp. 102–108.

Morton, Walter A., "The Structure of the Capital Market and the Price of Money," *American Economic Review*, XLIV (May 1954), pp. 440–459.

Robichek, A. A., and S. C. Myers, *Optimal Financing Decisions*. Englewood Cliffs, N.J.: Prentice-Hall, Inc., 1965.

Solomon, Ezra, *The Theory of Financial Management*. New York: Columbia University Press, 1963, Chapter XI.

7

Dividend Policy and Earnings Retention

> Obviously, the correct policy is to retain in the
> business each year that part of the profit and loss
> surplus which is necessary for its best interests
> and to distribute the remainder among the stock-
> holders to whom it really belongs.
> —J. H. Bonneville

The purpose of this chapter is to describe dividend policies and to raise the question of what the dividend policy of a firm should be, given the firm's objectives. Previously we adopted the position that management will accept only those projects expected to result in a positive or, at the worst, a neutral effect on wealth. Then from this point of view the dividend issue—as was true when funds sources and uses were considered—is a valuation problem. We must admit in advance that the question of what constitutes an optimal dividend policy has not been resolved. In fact, recent years have seen little measurable progress in our ability to deal with this issue operationally. On the other hand, dividend policy has been the subject of a great deal of scholarly research, and given adequate data and improved (unbiased) statistical studies, some progress in the direction of a general rule may yet be developed.

The reader may ask why we chose to devote a separate chapter to this issue. We have done so because we look on dividends and related issues as financial problems—problems that involve consideration of both funds sources and funds uses. Adequate treatment of dividends, it was felt, could not be given if the whole issue were treated incidentally or parenthetically to the two preceding chapters. Dividends are a distribution to the equity holder of retained earnings, and thus their payment—an outflow of cash—is to an extent a use of funds. But the "return" on dividend payments cannot be evaluated in the same manner as can other "investment" decisions, as the payment does not result in readily identifiable inflows, or returns to the firm. However, the objective—and hence the benchmark in deciding whether to make either an investment expenditure or a dividend distribution—is the same: What policy will maximize the wealth of the shareholder? The dividend decision when considered in relation to other financial decisions of the firm can affect both the firm's capital structure and its investment policy, and hence its risk, rate of growth, profitability, diversification, and so on.

INVESTOR REACTIONS TO DIVIDEND POLICIES

Dividend policy is a frequent item of discussion at stockholders' meetings. Seldom is there universal agreement among stockholders as to what it should be. Some insight into the source and validity of disagreement can be found by examining differences in stockholders' characteristics, circumstances, and motivations.

Stockholders differ with respect to age, sex, tax bracket, security, income, habits, preferences, attitudes toward risk, and responsibilities. Some are primarily concerned with the short run, others think in terms of long-range returns; still others seek a portfolio which balances their expectations over time. They have different utility functions, have access to different information, avail themselves of information in varying degrees, and act more or less intelligently on what information they do possess. One could say that investors are both rational and irrational. In fact, at times an important subset of the market may act in an irrational way; yet individual investors, recognizing this collective irrationality, may act rationally in response. In fact, we might expect this to happen, since a larger and larger percent of total trading activity is institutional activity.

One might ask why a stockholder would hold an investment in a company whose dividend policy differs from that which he thinks the company should follow. The answer, if the holder is rational, must be that, in spite of the fact that to him the current policy is nonoptimal, the security must offer either or both of the following: First, given the risk that he perceives, the security in question must promise (to him) either the greatest total return available from any security of this degree of risk, or the least amount of risk from any available security of this level of expected return. Second, the security may make a greater contribution to the value of his entire portfolio than would any other security.

DIVIDEND POLICIES OF U.S. FIRMS

Dividend policies vary widely between companies in different industries, even from company to company within the same industry, and also for firms within the same risk group.

Figure 7—1

Income and Dividient Payouts, All Active Corporate Returns*
Selected Years, 1929—67
(billions of dollars)

	Year										
	1929	1930	1935	1940	1945	1950	1955	1960	1965	1966	1967
Corporate profits after tax	8.6	2.9	2.6	7.2	9.0	24.9	27.0	26.7	45.2	49.3	47.2
Dividends	5.8	5.5	2.8	4.0	4.6	8.8	10.5	13.4	19.8	21.5	22.8
Undistributed profits.	2.8	-2.6	-0.2	3.2	4.4	16.0	16.5	13.2	25.4	27.8	24.4
Corporate capital consumption allowances	4.2	4.3	3.6	3.8	6.4	8.8	17.4	24.9	36.5	39.0	41.4
Dividend payout ratio	68.2	189.6	107.7	55.6	51.1	35.3	38.9	50.2	43.8	43.6	48.3

*Includes firms operating at a profit as well as those operating at a loss.

Source: United States Congress, Joint Economic Committee, 1968 Supplement to Economic Indicators.

Figure 7-1 shows the distribution of income among taxes, dividends and retained earnings for U.S. firms, from 1929 to 1967. It is interesting to note the relative stability of dividend payments as compared with earnings during the depression of the 1930's and in other periods of recessed business activity. This is not to say, however, that all corporations are able to maintain dividends when their incomes drop. To a significant degree the maintenance of dividends is a function of liquidity and the net balance of the money flows of the firm. As business slows down, many firms find that corporate liquidity mounts, and in some cases rapidly, as the firm converts inventories and receivables into cash and as it reduces, or ceases, to build up inventories and fixed assets. For other firms a decline in sales may result in a liquidity squeeze and, if severe enough, the results could be insolvency, reorganization, or bankruptcy. The dividend policies of firms during a period of business downturn are thus a function of the firms' liquidity. Some readers will undoubtedly note that a firm may have its most severe liquidity squeeze during a period of expansion. Why might this be true? What effect would this have on the firm's dividend policy?

The figures in Figure 7-1 reflect the preference many U.S. firms apparently have for paying dividends on some basis other than a fixed percentage of profits. One such policy, for example, would be to maintain dividends at a fixed level despite income fluctuations.

Earnings, taxes, dividends, and undistributed profits may be shown in

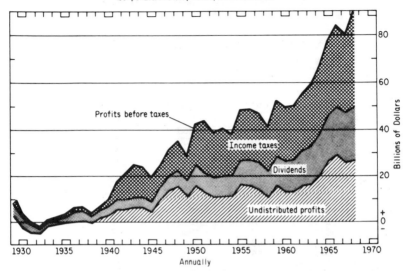

Figure 7-2
Corporate Profits, Taxes, and Dividends.

Source: Historical Chart Book, Board of Governors of the Federal Reserve System, 1969, p. 50.

a more interesting manner graphically, as in Figure 7-2. Could one conclude from this that the "best" dividend policy for any firm is equal to the average payout for all firms? To obtain some further insight into this question you may wish to plot the dividend payout ratios of particular firms in which you are interested. The results of such analyses are frequently surprising. For example, IBM, which sells on an extremely low dividend yield, nevertheless pays out around 40 percent of its earnings. Other growth firms, however, such as Litton Industries, pay out little or no dividends.

Let us look behind the highly aggregated figures that were the bases for Figures 7-1 and 7-2.

First we examine the payout ratio for the firms whose stock comprise the well known Dow Jones Industrial averages. On Figure 7-3 the average payout ratios for these important companies are shown. Note that these payout ratios are higher than for all active companies filing tax returns with the Internal Revenue Service. This would seem to indicate that large, listed firms have a higher payout than for smaller firms, listed or unlisted.

An interested reader may wish to divide the firms listed on the New York and American stock exchanges and then separate these firms into size classes to determine whether or not the average dividend payout bears a close

Figure 7-3

Payout Ratios for the Dow Jones Industrial Stocks
1929—67

Year	Dividends/Earnings Ratio	Year	Dividends/Earnings Ratio
1929	.63	1949	.54
1930	1.01	1950	.52
1931	2.05	1951	.61
1932		1952	.62
1933	1.61	1953	.59
1934	.93	1954	.61
1935	.71	1955	.60
1936	.70	1956	.69
1937	.76	1957	.60
1938	.82	1958	.71
1939	.67	1959	.60
1940	.64	1960	.66
1941	.65	1961	.71
1942	.69	1962	.64
1943	.64	1963	.56
1944	.68	1964	.67
1945	.63	1965	.53
1946	.55	1966	.55
1947	.49	1967	.55
1948	.49	1968	.60

(Source: Dow Jones and Company, Inc.)

relationship to size. *Query:* Should you divide firms by size of assets or size of income?

As a further probe into this question, we show in Figure 7-4 income, tax, dividend, and payout ratios for firms by broad industrial division and by size of net income. What does a study of these data indicate? First, there is a difference in the payout ratios between industries and, second, there is a variation in the payout ratios among those firms with larger incomes and those with smaller incomes. We have divided the firms into groups by size of income, and this is probably a fairly good proxy for size of assets.

The evidence from actual business practice seems to belie the existence of a "best" dividend policy, or at least would suggest that if such a policy exists it is not generally known or followed. Even companies that follow the same dividend policy may do so for different reasons and may be viewed differently by investors. A shareholder who has an investment preference for companies paying out a certain minimum percentage of earnings (say 50 percent), will find that the dividend yields of firms following such a policy will vary widely. This is explained by the fact that some shares sell at a higher price per dollar of dividend (and/or earnings) than others. One would expect this inasmuch as dividends are but part of the return to the shareholder, with capital gains, or losses, making up the other part of the return. As long as dividends are evaluated on a great many different bases by investors, there is no single dividend policy that will equate all companies in the eyes of these investors.

Even identical dividends can mean different things to different investors. For example, their after-tax yields can differ as the net yield is a function of the taxpayer's income tax rate. Dividends are taxed at the investor's marginal tax rate, after allowance for dividend exemption, and the gain, on sale if any, may be taxed as income or as a capital gain depending upon the holding period of the stock. Long-term capital gains, which are taxed at one-half the investor's income tax rate, up to a maximum rate of 25 percent, apply to securities held by an investor for more than six months. Short-term gains are taxed at the individual's marginal tax rate, whatever that rate may be, and this rate is levied on all gains from securities held for less than six months.

Despite varying investor reactions, there are some apparent regularities in corporate dividend policy. A myriad of dividend policies may be identified. In addition to the four common dividend policies described below there are regular cash dividends only; regular and extra cash dividends; cash and stock dividends; stock dividends only; no dividend at all, or any combination of all of these policies. However, for our purpose only four common dividend policies are described in relative detail.

FOUR DIVIDEND POLICIES

1. *A fixed percent of reported earnings.* Such a policy would result in a firm paying a fixed percent of its reported annual earnings as dividends. Since, for almost all firms, earnings can vary year to year, often through a relatively wide range, the result would be that dividends would vary in like proportions. Furthermore, if a firm pays dividends on a quarterly or even semiannual basis, the dividend can fluctuate from quarter to quarter, or period to period, as the earnings are reported. In practice, very few listed firms follow such a policy.

2. *A constant dividend, adjusted intermittently to bear a desired relationship to average level of earnings.* Firms that follow this policy are basically seeking to offer a constant payment to investors, making adjustments only in the event of significant fluctuations in earnings. The net effect of the intermittent adjustments is that dividends tend to bear a roughly fixed

Figure 7-4

Active Corporation Returns, 1963 (Other than firms filing under Form 1120 S)
Net Income, Income Subject to Tax, Investment Credit, Tax After Investment Credit, and Distribution to stockholders by industrial classifications
(000's)

Industrial Division and Size of Net Income or Deficit	Net Income	Income Subject to Tax[1]	Income Tax	Investment Credit[1]	Tax After Investment Credit[1]	Distributions to Stockholders Except in Stock	Payout Ratio Percent
All Industrial Divisions—Total	60,078	54,331	26,282	1,105	26,177	20,536	60.1
Under $25,000	3,525	3,016	864	64	799	703	25.8
$25,000 but under $1 million	12,672	11,399	5,073	213	4,860	2,397	30.1
$1 million but under $100 million	27,709	24,933	12,595	580	12,015	10,538	67.1
$100 million or more	16,172	14,975	7,750	248	7,502	6,898	79.6
Agriculture, Forestry, and Fisheries—Total	271	226	90	5	85	145	77.9
Under $25,000	54	42	12	2	10	23	52.3
$25,000 but under $1 million	148	120	48	2	46	98	96.1
$1 million but under $100 million	68	64	29	1	28	24	60.0
$100 million or more	—	—	—	—	—	—	—
Mining—Total	1,516	1,320	660	24	636	998	113.4
Under $25,000	30	22	6	2	4	10	38.5
$25,000 but under $1 million	226	171	77	9	68	151	95.6
$1 million but under $100 million	639	507	254	14	240	316	79.2
$100 million or more	620	620	323	—	323	521	175.4
Contract Construction—Total	1,057	912	369	24	344	123	17.2
Under $25,000	244	202	57	5	52	22	11.4
$25,000 but under $1 million	637	551	237	16	221	62	14.9
$1 million but under $100 million	176	160	74	3	71	39	37.1
$100 million or more	—	—	—	—	—	—	—
Manufacturing—Total	30,330	28,581	14,323	573	13,750	10,214	61.6
Under $25,000	522	440	126	19	107	76	18.3
$25,000 but under $1 million	4,732	4,412	1,162	30	1,132	389	10.8
$1 million but under $100 million	2,092	1,954	996	34	962	525	46.5
$100 million or more	291	282	146	—	146	133	91.7

Finance, Insurance, and Real Estate—Total	9,709	7,052	3,119	38	3,082	3,863	58.3
Under $25,000	1,036	894	256	4	252	343	43.7
$25,000 but under $1 million	2,784	2,309	953	15	938	806	43.7
$1 million but under $100 million	5,074	3,348	1,652	18	1,634·	2,343	68.1
$100 million or more	815	499	259	1	258	371	66.6
Transportation, Communication, Electric, Gas, and Sanitary Services—Total	9,342	9,013	4,570	331	4,239	3,734	73.2
Under $25,000	148	125	36	7	29	28	23.5
$25,000 but under $1 million	668	610	276	26	250	125	29.9
$1 million but under $100 million	4,937	4,734	2,432	198	2,234	2,356	87.2
$100 million or more	3,588	3,545	1,826	100	1,726	1,215	65.2
Wholesale and Retail Trade—Total	6,346	5,887	2,592	79	2,513	1,205	31.4
Under $25,000	1,134	1,003	289	16	273	158	18.3
$25,000 but under $1 million	2,819	2,646	1,162	30	1,132	389	23.1
$1 million but under $100 million	2,092	1,954	996	34	962	525	46.5
$100 million or more	—	—	—	—	—	—	—
Services—Total	1,500	1,336	558	30	528	252	25.9
Under $25,000	342	285	81	10	71	42	15.5
$25,000 but under $1 million	655	584	249	13	236	115	27.4
$1 million but under $100 million	503	467	227	7	220	95	33.6
$100 million or more	—	—	—	—	—	—	—
Nature of Business Not Allocable—Total	5	4	1	—	1	1	25.0
Under $25,000	5	4	1	—	1	—	—
$25,000 but under $1 million	—	—	—	—	—	—	—
$1 million but under $100 million	—	—	—	—	—	—	—
$100 million or more	—	—	—	—	—	—	—

1. Included in the total, but not in the detail are statistics for 28 taxable returns without net income. Tax on returns without net income occurs because of special provisions of the Internal Revenue Code applicable to insurance companies.

Source: Statistics of Income, 1963. Corporation Income Tax Returns. United States Treasury Department, Internal Revenue Service, Publication No. 16 (3-68).

relationship to earnings over time, although not so precisely as would be the case under (1) above. Still, as the average level of earnings changes, the size of the dividend will tend to be changed accordingly.

In times of rising earnings increased dividends are usually easy to justify even if one does not feel it is an optimal policy. On the other hand, as earnings fall from period to period, in a secular or long-trend sense, the payout ratio will increase unless the payments are adjusted downward. This policy can be defended if the downturn in earnings actually reflects the inability of the firm to invest in projects whose rate of return exceeds the cost of capital. If this is the case, then clearly all earnings, and all cash flows possible, should be paid, returned, to the owners in the form of income and/or liquidating dividends. Less-than-proportional payments, therefore, under the intermittent adjustment policy, would represent less than an optimal policy from the standpoint of investors, other things being equal.

3. *A constant annual dividend, related to an average level of earnings, adjusted both by the payment of extra dividends, and by changes, from time to time, in the annual dividend itself.* Such a policy, while similar to the above, differs to the extent that the firm is more closely, and with less of a lag, conforming to a target payout ratio. However, the policy is not the same as that of a constant percent of earnings (1) as the basic dividend is set, or fixed, and the extra dividend, since it cannot be negative, either leaves the annual dividend unchanged, or adds to it. (This does not mean that the annual dividend cannot be reduced, but it does mean that management views the annual dividend amount as a "fixed" charge or obligation in the event some predetermined payout is not reached.) Furthermore, extra dividends are usually paid only in those years when earnings exceed, or are expected to exceed, the annual dividend by a preconceived amount. For example, a firm may wish to pay out about 70 percent of earnings, but at the same time may want to maintain the basic dividend at some constant dollar figure. Under such circumstances, if the constant annual dividend represents say 50 percent of earnings, the additional 20 percent may be made up by the payment of extra dividends. Extra dividends allow management to recognize both year-to-year fluctuations in earnings, and long-term changes in earnings, provided conditions allow. In practice, a year-end extra and other extra dividends may be declared when the earnings of any period exceed the annual dividend requirement by some given amount. Thus a firm that expects average earnings of $1.43, and that had a target rate of 70 percent, would pay $1.00 per share in dividends. This rate would hold, then, even though earnings from year to year varied above and below this amount. If reported

earnings should exceed the fixed dividend requirement by a margin in excess of say 60 or 70 percent ($1.60 or $1.70), then this may be the signal to management to declare an extra dividend. (Note that management has a relatively high degree of control over the earnings that they report.) Whether or not the extra dividend were declared would depend on a number of factors, among which would probably be expected funds needs, the desired level of liquidity, expectations about future earnings levels, etc.

4. *An erratic dividend payout.* This is a catchall category used to describe those payout policies that do not relate to reported earnings in any definite way. For example, a firm may pay a dividend only when it has a large balance of idle cash. Or a closely held firm may declare a dividend in order to avoid the penalties for undue accumulation of income.[1] The bases on which sporadic dividends may be issued are many, and it is often hard to explain the actions of firms following this dividend policy without detailed knowledge of their inner workings.

In evaluating the four common dividend policies identified above, the first three, to a lesser or greater extent, involve some attempt to relate the size of dividends to the level of earnings. The erratic policy depends on a myriad of factors.

OPTIMAL DIVIDEND POLICY

If, for many firms, a target payout is an important consideration, this raises the question of what the "target" itself should be. In this sense, the way to evaluate whether any policy is optimal is by looking on the issue as a valuation problem—that is, by exploring the effect that target payout policies have on share values.

The Issue

In the preceding chapters we concluded that a firm should accept only those investments expected to add to the present value of the firm. In our analysis of fund sources we concluded that the firm should use that financing mix which maximized the firm's value. We now ask: Is there some distribution of earnings after taxes, given the investment decision and the capital structure, which, when all other things are equal, will maximize shareholder wealth?

The real world gives us conflicting answers to the above question. On

[1]See Secs. 531–537, 1954 U.S. Internal Revenue Code, as amended.

the one hand, there are companies that increase their dividends and experience an increase in the price of their stock. Conversely, there are those that raise their dividends and experience a drop in the price of their stock. Also, some firms pay out small dividends, and sell at very high price-earnings ratios; other firms pay rather generous dividends but sell at much lower price-earnings ratios. Coupled with our above observations about payout ratios among different firms, we are led to ask, where is the "golden mean"? Does dividend policy really have any effect on stock prices? Can we, in a world of uncertainty, measure the extent to which changes in stock prices are related exclusively to changes in dividend policy when so many other factors also influence stock values? Even with careful statistical studies, can bias be eliminated to the extent necessary to prove our developing theories? Oh for the ability to conduct controlled experiments, like the physical scientists!

Consistent with our previous line of thought, let us reword the question to ask: Is there a dividend policy, a pattern of dividend payments, such that, all other things being equal, the value of the firm to the shareholders is maximized? Any other type of problem concerning dividends, regardless of its specific importance, is viewed as lying outside the scope of this book.

In order to conceptualize this issue we examine briefly a number of the more relevant theories of dividend policy. In a survey such as this we cannot be exhaustive in our coverage. We do, however, attempt to give the reader a clear picture of the issue, the state of the art, and a valid set of conclusions.

Dividends and Firm Value

The value of a firm, or of any asset, is equal to the discounted present value of its expected stream of cash flows. In the already familiar but all too artificial world of certainty, where the outcome of future events is known, the value of a firm with an infinite life that pays a constant and perpetual dividend would be determined by simply finding the discounted present value of that income (cash) stream. Since the stream is known and certain, the discount rate used would be the riskless rate of interest. More precisely, the price per share, P_0 would be

$$P_0 = \sum_{t=1}^{\infty} \frac{e}{(1+r)^{\infty}}$$

where e equals net cash flows (constant in amount, perpetual in duration and certain), and r is the riskless rate of interest.

Is such a valuation approach useful in a more realistic situation where the firm's life may not be infinite, where the dividend is neither certain nor necessarily constant, and where the firm may terminate its life and pay a liquidating dividend? We could conclude that it is and state the formula as follows:

$$P_0 = \sum_{t=1}^{n} \frac{d_n}{(1+k)^n}$$

where P_O is the price per share at the beginning of any period just after the stock has gone ex-dividend, d_n is the expected operating (or liquidating) dividend, and k is the appropriate rate of discount. This rate of discount can be viewed as being made up of the riskless rate of interest, and some additional amount which is used to adjust for risk. This seems straightforward enough, and it appears that the transition from an artificial to the real world has been completed. But there are both operational difficulties and conceptual problems. The operational difficulties arise in attempting to estimate the elements of the income stream, their duration and their risk; the conceptual problem arises with respect to the handling of the discount rate. The source of the problem is that when you adjust for risk through the discount factor this amount is compounded over time, and we might well question whether this is reasonable.

One way to avoid this problem is to adjust for risk in the estimate of the periodic net cash flows, adjusting them to a "sure" amount, or certainty-equivalent. These amounts are then discounted at the riskless rate of interest in order to determine their present value.

Following this latter approach, let us again make use of the certainty-equivalent concept.[2] It is an amount that the maker of an investment would accept from an investment proposal as being equivalent to a sure or guaranteed payment of a stipulated amount. That is, an investor may expect a given investment proposal to yield a stream of net cash benefits of amounts n_1, n_2, etc., and estimate the variability of these flows, σ^2, as σ^2_1, σ^2_2, σ^2_3, etc. This variability is simply a measure of the dispersion of expected possible outcomes (net cash flows or earnings) around their mean value. The greater the variability the greater the risk. Since individuals have different attitudes about risk, we would expect that different individuals evaluating the same proposal may well arrive at different certainty-equivalents even though they all view the project the same in respect to expected earnings, their mean, and

---

[2]For discussion of the certainty-equivalent concept see *supra* pp. 69–72.

their variance. The difference then must be a function of their aversion from or attitudes about risk, and this could be expressed as a coefficient, say β. For risk averters, the value of this coefficient would be between 0 and .99 and for risk lovers would be greater than 1.00.

Since we are assuming that managers are risk-averse in our treatment, we would establish the certainty-equivalent of a finite stream of income as follows:

$$C_n = E_x - \beta\sigma^2$$

where C_n is the certainty-equivalent of a given element of an expected income stream, E_x is the mean expected value of this element, β the decision maker's risk-aversion coefficient, and σ^2 the variance, or variability, of the expected returns around their mean value, E_x.

The valuation formula would then appear as

$$V \quad \text{or} \quad P_0 = \sum_{t=1}^{n} \frac{C_n}{(1+r)^n}$$

where V or P_O is value or price, C_n the certainty-equivalent of the income stream in period n, and r the riskless rate of interest.

We have already established that in a world of certainty, the value of a firm, whose earnings are constant and perpetual, and which pays out all of its earnings as dividends, is equal to

$$V = \frac{d}{(1+r)} + \frac{d}{(1+r)^2} + \cdots + \frac{d}{(1+r)^\infty},$$

or

$$= \frac{d}{r}$$

Could we also show that in this world of certainty, where the firm's re-investment rate must also be equal to r, the riskless rate, that dividend policy would be a matter of indifference? Would this be true even if the dividend payment was zero? We can answer this question in terms of a model developed by James E. Walter.[3] His formula is as follows:

[3]James E. Walter, "Dividend Policies and Common Stock Prices," *Journal of Finance*, 9 (March 1956), pp. 29–41.

$$P = \frac{D + \dfrac{R_a}{R_c}(E - D)}{R_c}$$

where P = market price per share of common stock
D = dividends per share
R_a = return earned on the investment of the firm
R_c = the market capitalization rate
E = earnings per share

Using this formula to answer our question we would find the following if $R_a = R_c = .05$ and if we let $E = \$6$ and $D = $ a range of values from $\$2$ to $\$6$.

$$P = \frac{2 + 1(6 - 2)}{.05} = \frac{6}{.05} = 120$$

$$= \frac{6 + 1(6 - 6)}{.05} = \frac{6}{.05} = 120$$

As we see, for any value of D, given E and given that $R_a = R_c$, the value of the shares is constant. We will leave it to the student to determine that if $R_a > R_c$, that the stock price is maximized when $D = 0$ and that if $R_a < R_c$, stock price is maximized when $D = E$.

This formula is a simple capitalization approach and leads to the conclusion that dividend policy should be determined exclusively on the basis of the firm's investment opportunities. Furthermore, it assumes that the capitalization rate applied to a dollar of earnings is the same as the capitalization rate applied to a dollar of retained earnings, after the latter has been adjusted by the ratio of R_a to R_c. When this ratio is 1, the resultant formula really begs the question, and when $R_a/R_c \neq 1$, we cannot be at all sure that the ratio R_a/R_c adjusts the retained earnings to a level that will really reflect the market valuation of retained earnings.

The value of a firm, V_t, whose expected dividends are $\hat{d}_t$ per share, and which has n_t shares outstanding in period t, is

$$V_t = \frac{\hat{d}_t \, n_t + \hat{v}_t + 1}{1 + k}$$

More simply, by setting $d_t n_t$ equal to D_t, we have

$$V_t = \frac{D_t + v_{t+1}}{(1+k)}$$

In words, the value of a firm at the beginning of any period t, just after the stock has gone ex-dividend, is equal to the discounted present value of expected dividends during the period, if any, and the expected value of the stock V_t at the end of the period.

From the standpoint of the firm's dividend policy, the above formula raises the critical issue of whether the amount of dividends per se affects the value of the firm. That is, in light of investors' perceptions of the firm's investment opportunities, and in respect to investors' opportunity costs and their attitudes toward risk, does a dollar of retained earnings have the same effect on price as does a dollar of dividends?

The usefulness of this formula can be expanded if we allow for external financing. Also, since our objective is to determine the value or influence of dividend policy per se on stock prices, we must be careful to keep all other factors constant. For example, a growing firm will have a number of investment opportunities available during any given time period, and we must not let the level of investments I change as a function of dividend policy when we are evaluating the impact of the dividends.

Following a ground-breaking research paper by Miller and Modigliani[4] on dividend policy, we can show the neutrality or irrelevance of dividend policy through their model which is based on the following key assumptions:

1. Rational investors
2. Perfect knowledge
3. Perfect capital markets
4. Costless transactions
5. No tax differential between income (on dividends) and capital gains (gains from sale of stock, whether long or short term)
6. A given investment policy that holds irrespective of the dividend payout
7. And, at least initially, that all investors know with certainty all future investments of the firm and their profitability

As above, we have

---

[4]Merton H. Miller and Franco Modigliani, "Dividend Policy, Growth and the Valuation of Shares," *Journal of Business*, XXXIV (October 1961), pp. 411–433.

$$V_t = \frac{D_t + v_{t+1}}{(1+k)}$$

However, given the assumptions of the Miller and Modigliani model, we can drop the expectational notation and concept since perfect knowledge and resulting certainty are assumed.

Then, letting I equal the total dollar value of new investments to be made during the year, X the total net profit of the firm for the year, and m the total number of shares sold by the firm at the end of period 1 at price P_1, a price formula that does not include dividends is developed. First, assume that in order to make total investments I, given the total dividends during the first period D_1, that the firm sells m shares for which it receives mP_1. The amount mP_1 that was raised and that needed to be raised given the investment needs and the dividends, is

$$mP_1 = I - (X - nD_1)$$

Since new shares have been sold during the period, the total value of shares at the beginning of the period must be adjusted to reflect these new claims. Thus, where $e =$ net cash flows as previously defined,

$$nP_0 = \left[\frac{1}{(1+e)}\right]\left[nD_1 + (n+m)P_1 - mP_1\right]$$

This formula now reflects the fact that the total value of all outstanding shares at the beginning of any period, say t, is equal to the discounted present value of all dividends accruing to those shares during the period plus the value of all shares outstanding at the end of the period minus the value of those shares issued during the period, at the assumed terminal price, P_1.

Since it has been established that $mP_1 = I - (X - nD_1)$, we can substitute this value in our basic valuation formula, obtaining

$$nP_0 = \left[\frac{1}{(1+e)}\right]\left[nD_1 + (n+m)P_1 - I + X - nD_1\right]$$

Canceling out the nD_1 terms leaves

$$nP_0 = \left[\frac{1}{(1+e)}\right]\left[(n+m)P_1 - I + X\right]$$

Since price has been expressed such that dividends do not appear in the valuation formula, it can be argued that dividend policy is irrelevant. However, this position is not entirely consistent with the way in which stock prices are established, for the reasons set forth below.

In the above discussion, the dividend is treated as a secondary consideration, since the dividend is that amount left after the investment decision is made. In this case the rate of return on incremental investments determined the investment policy and the amount of the investment, and thus determined both dividend policy and the price of the shares.

REINVESTMENT OF EARNINGS AND/OR OUTSIDE FINANCING—NO GROWTH

When outside financing is introduced, it can be shown—provided one is willing to accept certain assumptions critical to the proof—that dividend policy has no effect on the price of a share of stock. This means that the investment decision is *the* determinant of price.

A proof of this position is as follows. If a firm with constant and perpetual earnings pays out all of its earnings as dividends, then its stock price P equals E/k, which, in turn, equals D/k. If, however, a firm retains part of its earnings b and invests these at its cost of capital k, and if b is defined as "a constant percent of its earnings," then

$$P_0 = \frac{1}{1+k}(D+P_1) = \left[\frac{\dfrac{(1-b)kE}{k+1}}{\dfrac{k}{1}} \right] + \left[\frac{\dfrac{bEk}{k+1}}{k} \right] + \left[\frac{\dfrac{E}{k+1}}{k} \right]$$

$$= \left[\frac{\dfrac{(1-b)\,Ek + E + bEk}{k+1}}{k} \right] = \left[\frac{\dfrac{Ek+E}{k+1}}{k} \right] = \left[\frac{\dfrac{E(k+1)}{k+1}}{k} \right] = \frac{E}{k}$$

Thus, investing any part of earnings in any period, at the cost of capital, has no effect on share prices, and P_0, as was the case when all earnings were paid out as dividends, is equal to E/k. Similarly, if the company paid out all of its earnings, but raised the additional capital by selling stock exactly at its current price then the same result would obtain. In this case,

$$P_0 = \frac{E}{1+k} \left[\frac{\dfrac{E}{1+k}}{k} \right] + \left[\frac{\dfrac{bEk}{1+k}}{k} \right] - \left[\frac{\dfrac{bEk}{1+k}}{k} \right] = \left[\frac{\dfrac{Ek+E}{1+k}}{k} \right] = \frac{E}{k}$$

Reinvestment of Earnings and Growth—A Simple Model

Now let us assume that the company invests a portion of its earnings b at a rate of return r which is greater than k. If no outside financing is used, and provided we restrict our model to an all-equity company (completely free of debt), then the overall effect of retention on valuation, under simple growth conditions, can be shown as

$$P_0 = \left[\frac{(1-b)\,E}{1+k} \right] + \left[\frac{\dfrac{E}{1+k}}{k} \right] + \left[\frac{\dfrac{bEr}{1+k}}{k} \right]$$

$$= \left[\frac{\dfrac{(1-b)Ek + E + bEk + bE\,(r-k)}{k+1}}{k} \right] = \frac{E}{k} + \left[\frac{\dfrac{bE(r-k)}{1+k}}{k} \right]$$

If we let

$$I = \left[\frac{\dfrac{bE(r-k)}{1+k}}{k} \right]$$

then $P_0 = \dfrac{E}{k} + I$, where I is greater than zero. Thus, when the company invests a portion of its earnings in a project which promises a rate of return greater than the cost of capital, the price rises by an amount I.

Should the company wish to raise the funds by selling stock instead of financing the project out of retained earnings, the same result obtains, if we assume that the new stock is sold at its existing price—e.g., that new investors require only a rate of return on their investment equal to k and that they agree with management on the earnings prospect of the newly issued stock. In this case

$$P_0 = \frac{E}{1+k} + \left[\frac{\dfrac{E}{1+k}}{k} \right] + \left[\frac{\dfrac{bEr}{1+k}}{k} \right] - \left[\frac{\dfrac{bEk}{1+k}}{k} \right]$$

$$= \left[\frac{\dfrac{Ek}{1+k} + \dfrac{E}{1+k} + \dfrac{bEk}{1+k} + \dfrac{bE(r-k)}{1+k} - \dfrac{bEk}{1+k}}{k} \right]$$

$$= \left[\frac{\dfrac{Ek+E}{1+k}}{k} + \frac{\dfrac{bE(r-k)}{1+k}}{k} \right] = \frac{E}{k} + I$$

The Real World of Uncertainty

In an uncertain world with taxes where firms may finance part or all of new investments out of new issues of stock, new investors might not evaluate the rate of return of the proposed investment as favorably as does the management; therefore the effective rate of return demanded k' is greater than k. Also, in the real world with taxes, stockholders cannot reinvest their entire dividend income in other investments, since taxes consume a portion of these earnings. Furthermore, since capital gains are taxed at lower rates than for ordinary income, investors should prefer, if given a choice, to take their "dividends" by selling stock rather than by taking cash dividends. If this is so, it must be concluded that corporations are not acting in the best interests of their stockholders when they both pay a dividend and issue new stock to finance new investments. This appears especially true when a company must issue new shares of stock at a dollar value less than the current market price in order to induce the additional investment, as this implies that new investors require a greater return than present stockholders.

In this respect, from Modigliani and Miller's article one can make an unsettling inference about U.S. securities markets.[5] Investors, they argue, seem to place a premium on stocks which have a steady dividend payout that is a

[5]*Ibid.*

high percentage of the company's income. This is viewed as unexplainable, "irrational" behavior, and the only hope is that investors can learn from experience and/or by reading articles such as theirs.

Another explanation of why stockholders prefer dividends is that there are brokerage fees and transfer taxes. It is very expensive to sell small amounts of stock to produce a dividend equivalent through stock sales. Likewise, a certainty model need not hold in an uncertain world where dividends and the manner in which they are issued are considered significant pieces of information about the future earning power of a corporation. A high dividend exhibiting small but steady growth may be looked on as indicative of a stable company. On the other hand, a similar corporation following an erratic dividend policy may be looked on as a more risky investment. As such, two corporations which on other grounds might be placed in the same business risk class may be viewed differently if the stability of dividends is used to evaluate risk. Likewise, low dividends may cause investors to conclude that maybe the earnings picture is in actuality not as rosy as portrayed on the income statement. Thus in a certain world, dividend policy should have no effect on the price of a share of stock. In an uncertain world, on the other hand, this may not necessarily be the case.

Growth stocks, such as Eastman Kodak, Litton Industries, Polaroid, and Xerox, are able to overcome the stigma of low or nonexistent dividends because of their growth and growth potential. Investors buy these stocks looking forward to the future rather than to the present, and frequently in a portfolio which takes account of the present in other ways. As their potential growth becomes realized growth, then it is logical to assume that investors will place more weight on dividends. IBM, which is still considered a growth stock, as we mentioned previously, pays out about 40 percent of its earnings as dividends, as compared with an average of about 70 percent for leading listed firms. For all U.S. firms, large and small, listed and unlisted, however, the average is about 30 percent, a factor with interesting wealth-maximization implications.

Thus in the real world a reasonable contention is that dividend policy does affect the price of a share of stock because it provides information about future earnings and dividends rather than being itself a causal factor. General Motors provides a good example. In the mid-1960's, when General Motors announced a cut of 25 cents in its special dividend, the price of the stock immediately dropped two points. One could argue that this represented an adjustment in demand for the stock for those who had expected the special dividend as likely to continue as in the past, and that a sales decline had induced the drop. But previously G.M. had reported that earnings were not keeping up with their 1965 pace, sales in April had declined from the previous year, and G.M. was cutting back production. For those concerned with earnings and the special dividend, such information should also have served as bases to adjust demand. Possibly it did, and such investors may have adjusted their holdings steadily over time and in advance of the final earnings report. But the dividend cut was concrete, timely evidence that finally confirmed what was only previously suspected. As such, it could be argued that the dividend cut caused a simultaneous reevaluation, by a significant number of investors, of the future earnings prospects of the company and so the price declined.

Another link between dividend policy and share values stems from the fact that some stockholders may be more interested in short-run than in long-run earnings. Forecasting earnings for one year in advance is tenuous, but nonetheless defensible estimates can be made. Forecasting earnings and growth 10 or 20 years in advance, however, is a rough guess at best. Thus an investor, under uncertainty, remains cautious about the future; he may therefore give greater weight to expectations concerning present dividends than to beliefs as to what the trend in price and dividends might be over the long run.

Finally, in this argument it should be recognized that investors do not always act rationally, as assumed above, nor do they always assume that other investors are rational. An investor may buy an "undervalued" stock even though he expects the price to drop further, and he may sell an "overvalued" stock even though he expects that the market will continue to rise. Moreover, the "stop" order would appear completely irrational in a certain world. Modigliani and Miller suggest buying when the price drops, and selling when the price rises—not vice versa. Such a procedure is defensible only in an uncertain world, or when the behavior of investors is not considered rational.

Dividends and Cost of Capital

Gordon contends that investors prefer present dividends to future growth.[6] Although his contention may be correct, his proof is inadequate. Gordon's proof generally goes as follows. Let us assume that a company pays out all of its earnings as dividends and that its earnings are constant for perpetuity, so that the price of its shares equals its earnings capitalized at the cost of capital, or $P_O = E/k$. One day the company announces that it will not pay any dividend that year, but will reinvest it at the cost of capital.

---

[6]Myron J. Gordon, *The Investment, Financing, and Valuation of the Corporation* (Homewood, Ill.: Richard D. Irwin, Inc., 1962), pp. 181–184.

After that they will pay out all of their earnings $E = kE + E$ each year for perpetuity. Under Modigliani and Miller's theory, this will not affect the price per share, as

$$P_0 = \left[\frac{E + kE}{\frac{1 + k}{k}} \right] = \frac{E}{k}$$

But let us further assume, Gordon continues, that when the company announces it will retain all of its earnings for a given year that the cost of capital for this company rises to $k' > k$.[7] Thus the price of the stock will decline, for

$$P'_0 = \left[\frac{E + Ek}{\frac{1 + k'}{k'}} \right] < P_0 \left[\frac{E + Ek}{\frac{1 + k}{k}} \right]$$

In the above example the price of the stock declined because the cost of capital rose. Since the cost of capital rose when the company decided to retain all of its earnings for that year, it obviously, to Gordon, rose because the company put off paying dividends farther into the future. Since future earnings are more risky than present earnings, the cost of capital increased. Thus dividend policy affects the price of stock, as stockholders value present dividends more than future dividends.

Modigliani and Miller agree that the price of the shares of stock declines, but for a different reason.[8] In their view, the price would decline because the company invested at $k < k'$, where k' is the new cost of capital. Just as when the price of stock increases as investments are made which have a rate of return greater than the cost of capital, so does it decline when investments are made at less than the cost of capital. Note that this makes the decline a result of investment policy rather than dividend policy.

Modigliani and Miller are correct if it is assumed that the rise for k to k' was a general rise in the cost of capital, and if they are referring only to the price decline caused by the difference between paying a dividend and the present value of the earnings attributable to the investment. But the price

---

[7]Myron J. Gordon, "Optimal Investment and Financing Policy," *Journal of Finance*, 18 (May 1963), p. 267.

[8]Morton H. Miller and Franco Modigliani, *op. cit.*, p. 425.

declines also because the originally expected future earnings are now discounted at a higher cost of capital. There is thus an apparent discrepancy between the Modigliani and Miller and Gordon viewpoints, for we can reconcile the objection of the former and still show a price decline.

Let us assume that the company invested its earnings at a rate of return k', the new cost of capital. A price decline is still the logical consequence:

$$P'_0 = \left[\frac{E + Ek'}{\frac{1 + k'}{k'}} \right] = \frac{E}{k'} < \frac{E}{k'} = P_0$$

The stockholders lost nothing by the investment, yet the price still declined because the cost of capital rose; and the cost of capital rose, Gordon contends, because of dividend policy.

Gordon's argument is circular. What he says in effect is: "Let us assume that investors raise the cost of capital for a company when it retains earnings instead of paying them out as dividends." The only way it can be proven that investors do raise the cost of capital when companies retain earnings instead of paying them out as dividends is to empirically test the hypothesis holding all other factors equal. Unfortunately, one cannot hold all other factors equal, but it may be possible to control for extraneous factors if a large enough sample is used, and if such a sample can be found.

One other problem with Gordon's analysis, even if it is empirically correct, is that what he refers to is essentially a short-run phenomenon. At the end of the period, when the company resumes paying dividends, the cost of capital should then decline from k' to k. By then the company should be in the same position relative to future dividends as if it had not retained the earnings. Thus even though the price of the stock may decline when a company retains all its earnings to invest at a rate of return greater than the cost of capital, it is still to the long-run benefit of the stockholders to make the investment.

The Dividend as Information

The relationship between price and dividends is not a simple function. In the real world, investors neither know the value of future earnings, nor are they necessarily aware of what present or past earnings are. Publicly released accounting statements are prepared according to "generally accepted accounting principles." Generally accepted accounting principles allow a company to use a myriad of different accounting methods in determining income, and, in addition, certification requirements and liability consequences are such that managements do not reveal their expectations to the stockholders, at least not through the certified statement. A company can use straight-line or accelerated methods of depreciation, different lives for identical assets, FIFO or LIFO inventory-valuation methods, the purchase or pooling of interest method of accounting for mergers, and so on. In some cases, following accepted accounting principles can obscure income.

Assume a company owns 1,000 shares of the XYZ Corporation which it bought for $5 per share, and that at the end of the year the stock is selling in the market at $50 per share. If the company sells this stock, it earns $45,000, assuming, of course, that the market has some depth at the currently quoted prices. If it keeps the stock, it earns nothing, and the value of the stock remains at $5 per share on the company's books.

We might also mention another frequently encountered problem in the interpretation of income statements: The accounting that is made for leased assets. For example, a USDA study showed that leased assets comprised 39 percent of the capital of supermarkets, compared with only 4 percent for food processors. Calculating return on capital with total assets being the measure of invested capital revealed that the supermarkets had a higher rate of return. However, when the capitalized value of leased assets was included in the calculations, the food processors had a return of 12 percent, compared to a 10 percent return for the supermarkets.[9] From this it follows that ratios of profits to capital are overstated if no consideration is given to leased assets—only one of the host of pitfalls that interfere with truly "rational" investment analysis.

Thus in investment analysis some financial statements have little if any meaning, and the investor may have little or no reliable information on company earnings. This may be true even after adjustments have been made by professional analysts who often differ in their opinions as to the nature of such adjustments. If this is the case, is it any wonder that dividends are looked on as providing important additional data about the firm, and thus are used to help evaluate corporate financial statements? Unlike the many measures that might be made of what a firm *might* do, dividends are a concrete reflection of what the firm is doing in the way of providing returns to its investors.

[9]Stephen J. Hiemstra, "Lease-Financing and Returns to Capital of Food Marketing Firms," *Agricultural Economics Research,* 14 (January 1962), pp. 18–29.

If the dividend announced by the company is exactly what the investor expected it to be, it may be argued that little new information is generated. If investors expect a company to double its dividend payout, and the company does double its dividends, investors merely confirm their expectations. On the other hand, when the dividend differs from expectations, this in itself is additional information. If a company unexpectedly raises its dividends, or raises them more than was expected, this represents a fact to which investors must react. Under such circumstances, investors may well decide that the dividend was raised because the company expects even higher earnings. As such, investors could revise upwards the expected earnings for the company, and this could lead to an increase in the price paid per share. On the other hand, an increased payout ratio for a firm could be interpreted as evidence that the company has run out of profitable new investment opportunities, and is thus paying out greater dividends. Estimates of future growth in earnings could therefore be revised downward and, as investors act on these new expectations, the price of the stock could drop, other things being equal. At the same time, another company may lower its dividends, and investors may interpret this to mean that earnings expectations are poor; again, a drop in share prices may be the likely consequence.

In conclusion, we suggest that the amount of the dividend itself does not directly influence the price paid for the stock in the manner that an investment model under certainty might lead one to assume, but that the information inferred from a changed dividend reflects expectation as to the company's future earning potential, and thus indirectly influences the price of its shares. In like fashion, changes in the rate of dividend payout also cause investors to attempt to interpret the rationale behind such changes and to take action based on the informational content of such a move.

SUMMARY AND CONCLUSIONS

In this chapter we have analyzed investment models and theories of investor behavior as they relate to the search for an optimal dividend policy. These are the questions we started with: (1) What effect does dividend policy have on (a) the price of a share of stock, and (b) on the cost of capital? (2) Is there an optimal dividend policy? These questions have been left unanswered in terms of the real world. The theoretical models cited help reveal what independent variables must be measured and trace out the effect of changes in dividend policy on firm value. However, it is a fallacy to set dividend policy on the assumption that such models govern investor behavior if indeed significant numbers of investors make decisions on other grounds. In this sense such models could be categorized as theoretically defensible but operationally worthless. Instead, one must anticipate investor reactions not as they *ought* to be, but as they are *likely* to be.

In the development of a rational basis on which to determine an optimal dividend policy, further advances, both theoretical and empirical, will require refinements and progress in at least the following areas:

1. A separation of the time value of money from the treatment of uncertainty or subjectively assigned risk must be accomplished.
2. A meaningful measure of the extent to which the universe of stockholders is partitioned, if at all, and a determination of whether particular subsets of investors do hold stocks of companies that have particular dividend policies. The issue appears on the surface to be one that could be successfully attacked, for example, through the use of discriminate analysis from which one could obtain a profile of those investors who hold particular stocks. However, the measurement will be complicated by the facts that (a) portfolio construction and (b) trade-offs between a desired dividend policy and a desirable growth rate, may lead important investors to hold stocks of widely varying dividend policies.
3. Some technique is needed to develop an assessment and measurement of the informational content of dividend amounts, dividend payout ratios, and changes in dividend payouts.

Lest the reader lose heart and conclude that in this respect he is confronted by a hopeless task, it should be stated that in recent years firms have made considerable advances in assessing the reactions of their customers to the goods and services they offer. Here it may well be that the finance manager can learn from his counterpart who directs the firm's marketing operations. Consumers react to the products offered by a firm, and in one sense a firm's externally offered securities can be viewed as a product. Just as product features (size, color, shape, price) are subject to evaluation, often of a subtle nature, by individual consumers, so are its financial offerings subject to investor evaluation. In the development of product policy and in the analysis of consumer behavior one finds the simplifying analytic concept of market segmentation used in conjunction with the time-consuming techniques of depth analysis and motivation research. There are no compelling reasons why such approaches might not also be applied to the area of financial management, where one of the key considerations is the collective reaction of the multisector investment market to dividend policy.

SUGGESTED REFERENCES

Brigham, Eugene F., and Myron J. Gordon, "Leverage, Dividend Policy and the Cost of Capital," *Journal of Finance* 23 (March, 1968) pp. 85–103.

Friend, Irwin, and Marshall Puckett, "Dividends and Stock Prices," *American Economic Review* 54 (September, 1964). See especially pp. 661–663.

Gordon, Myron J., "Some Estimates of the Cost of Capital to the Electric Utility Industry, 1954–57: Comment," *American Economic Review* 42 (December 1967), p. 1267.

Lintner, John, "Distribution of Incomes of Corporations Among Dividends, Retained Earnings and Taxes," *American Economic Review* 46 (May, 1956) pp. 97–113.

Modigliani, Franco, and Merton Miller, "The Cost of Capital, Corporation Finance, and the Theory of Investment," *American Economic Review* 48 (June, 1958) pp. 261–297.

8

Managerial Behavior and Decisions of the Firm

> Labor can do nothing without capital, capital
> nothing without labor, and neither labor nor capi-
> tal can do anything without the guiding genius of
> management.—W. L. Mackenzie King

In this chapter we are concerned with the manner in which managers act and interact, and how this affects the decisions that are made for a firm. Specifically we are interested in the finance, marketing, and production managers, both individually and as a group. Our ultimate concern is how decisions made with respect to the major functional areas ultimately give a direction to the firm's activity as a whole. Consideration of this issue ultimately leads us to take a systemic view of the firm's activities.

FIRST—A LOOK BACKWARD

Previously we pointed out that the managers in the various functional areas deal with different types of problems, but that ultimately a coordination of their efforts is necessary. And if the three managers differ materially in background and outlook, then problems in the latter area are compounded.

In our attempt to identify the person of the finance manager in the firm, we found that this position was described by a great many different job titles. Additional variance is introduced by the fact that there are a wide range of individual differences which must be taken into account among persons filling the positions in question. The finance manager may have a background in investments, banking, credit, law, accounting, or data processing—to name a few likely possibilities. The production manager is likely to be an engineer, although many have less formal education or come from other backgrounds. Of all the three it used to be easiest to characterize the marketing manager. Traditionally, field sales experience led into this position;

however, the recent separation of marketing from selling has served to open this job to persons with a wide range of corporate experience.

The functional managers' interaction takes place given the fact that they are simultaneously filling at least two roles: one as individuals and one as representatives of a definable portion of the firm's total activity. Even though individual differences may lead to differences in their behavior, typically a great deal of their common frame of reference stems from the fact that their prior striving has resulted in their attainment of managerial status. It is also reasonable to assume in most cases that they hope one outcome of their present efforts will be the attainment of even greater responsibilities and higher-level positions within the firm.

Another common denominator that links them is the fact that everything they do gets translated into financial terms. The system of which they are a part and which they both accept and influence is one defined in dollars-and-cents equivalents. This reiteration of the pervasiveness of the finance function is not designed to unduly elevate its importance. For without production or markets the firm does not exist.

But in their interaction the functional managers act as spokesmen for greatly different types of activity. This leads to preferences and to decisions that relate not only to the firm as a whole but also to the particular problems they face in their own spheres of influence. Managers do not derive their authority from any divine intercession; instead, their ability to implement ideas and maintain control is very much a function of the extent to which they are tolerated by their subordinates. One cannot assume that a manager will necessarily put firm interests above those of department or self. Indeed, one major source of corporate crises is when the interests of the firm and its subsystems are not readily reconcilable.

Previously we argued that wealth maximization be adopted as the end to which corporate activities be directed. It does not matter at this point whether firms do indeed maximize their wealth, or whether they should do so. We are merely continuing to make this a tangible assumption on which we have built one model, which, if one chooses, can be compared with others that might be developed if this assumption were relaxed.

How Wealth is Maximized

To this point, we have considered how management should conceptualize its problems if wealth maximization is the objective. Presumably there are revenues and costs attached to finance, marketing, and production activities, and the wealth maximization objective is served if over time they are managed so as to result in the greatest contribution to wealth from each area, provided tendencies toward suboptimization are avoided. This chapter is concerned with the practical problems encountered by the functional managers as they proceed toward the above objective. To start in this direction, let us first consider how business decisions are made.

DECISION-MAKING BEHAVIOR

In examining the decision-making behavior of business executives, we start with the assumption that they are rational beings. This merely assumes that an attempt is made to calculate the utilities attached to various alternatives, and that the one chosen is the one with the greatest utility attached. But what problems are encountered by businessmen seeking to be "rational" when they are faced by the complex types of business situations analyzed in the previous chapters? The individual's reaction to complexity in decision making has been tentatively explored by March and Simon, who drew on a great deal of published literature in their discussion of the cognitive limits to rationality. By way of conclusion they state:

> Because of the limits of human intellective capacities in comparison with the complexities of the problems that individuals and organizations face, rational behavior calls for simplified models that capture the main features of a problem without capturing all its complexities.[1]

Thus in evaluating how businessmen act, one departure from the idea of perfect rationality has been proposed—the idea that decisions are made in terms of a model incorporating a reduced number of variables, but which hopefully captures the main features of the situation.

Another departure specified by March and Simon is the tendency to seek "satisfactory" rather than the "best" solutions to business problems.[2] Logically, one can offer support for such a view along several lines:

1. Frequently, the unknowns affecting a situation are so many, and can at best be defined with limited precision, so that it becomes very difficult to distinguish among feasible alternatives.

[1]James G. March and Herbert A. Simon, *Organizations* (New York: John Wiley & Sons, Inc., 1958), p. 169.
[2]*Ibid.*, p. 46.

2. The cost attached to the development of more precise information often exceeds the value which may reasonably be gained through use of that information. Furthermore, it is by no means a certainty that further attempts at precision in specifications will be successful.

3. At least in the United States over the post-World War II period, the general munificence of the economy has not made finding the optimal solution a necessary condition for survival and/or a satisfactory level of profit.

4. In many business situations there are heavy penalties attached to doing nothing. Thus a timely, less-than-optimal solution may in the long run be of greater benefit to the firm than a more carefully researched but untimely one.

Kenneth Boulding has also recognized this situation by developing a theory of the firm which uses *homeostasis* as the mechanism of decision making. Certain relationships within the business—balance-sheet ratios, for example—are somehow established as ideal, and the mechanism of the firm is so set up that significant deviations from these standard relationships will bring into play counteracting forces designed to pull the relationships back to normal. There is simply no room for a profit maximizing goal in such a model as this. Nothing is maximized. Variables, included among them profit itself, are simply restricted to certain ranges of fluctuation which are "satisfactory." The implementation of such a model therefore leads in the direction of "satisfactory" profits rather than maximum profits.[3]

A great deal of comment is to be found to the effect that the computer will ultimately lead businessmen to more rational solutions (a) because of its ability to handle large numbers of variables and analyze their relationship, and (b) because of its speed. The counterargument is to point to the benefits derived from human experience. Ultimately, the issue breaks down to whether a computer can assimilate such experience, apply it to specific problems, and augment its problem-solving capacities in the process. At first glance, if the view that decisions are actually made in terms of relatively simple models is reasonably correct, then capturing such models within the confines of a computer program presents no special problems, provided the precise form of the model can be specified in the first place. But this ignores an alternate view of the decision-making process, one for which a consid-

---

[3]Kenneth E. Boulding, "Implications for General Economics of More Realistic Theories of the Firm," *American Economic Review,* 32 (May 1952), p. 40.

erable body of supporting empirical evidence has been offered by the so-called "transactional" psychologists.[4]

They attack more traditional work in perception as being too heavily involved with analysis of objective and physiological influences on decisions, and not enough concerned with the large body of mainly interdependent subjective influences affecting the individual's awareness of the world about him. The transactionalist views the decision maker's awareness of the situation as the result of a complicated weighing process the individual goes through as his mind takes into account both the nature of the stimulus and his past experience in identical or similar situations. They argue that the integration of these elements, in number effectively running into the thousands, may be accomplished within a fraction of a second, and more often than not at a level other than the conscious. Furthermore, the awareness that emerges is not derived independently of the individual's purposes at the moment, or of his expectations as to what his future purposes may prove to be. This opens the door to the introduction of a whole series of personal and subjective factors which can and do affect the decision that is made for any given set of facts (stimuli).

Even though it is not possible to come to any clear agreement as to how business decisions are made, or how they should be made, we still have to face the fact that individual and collective actions by managers in the functional areas tend to move business firms in certain directions.[5] In considering top-level decision making as it affects resource allocation, let us first examine the types of things that (it is reasonable to believe) affect whatever alternative is chosen.

Differences in Attitudes Toward Risk

Several interesting attempts to evaluate businessmen's attitudes toward risk have been undertaken in the recent past.[6] On the basis of an experimental

---

[4]For an idea of the contributions to this point of view, see Franklin P. Kilpatrick (ed.), *Human Behavior: the Transactional Point of View* (Hanover, N.H.: Institute for Associated Research, 1952); and Franklin P. Kilpatrick (ed.), *Explorations in Transactional Psychology* (New York: New York University Press, 1961).

[5]For one discussion of how this leads to conflict, see H. J. Hindricks, "Finance on the Frontier," *Financial Executive*, 32 (March 1964), pp. 51–54.

[6]Paul E. Green, "Risk Attitudes and Chemical Investment Decisions," *Chemical Engineering Progress* (January 1963), p. 35; C. Jackson Grayson, Jr., *Decisions Under Certainty* (Boston: Harvard University, Division of Research, 1960); Ralph O. Swalm, "Utility Theory—Insights into Risk Taking," *Harvard Business Review*, 44 (November–December 1966), pp. 123–138.

research design involving a series of hypothetical two-outcome gambles expressed in terms of return on investment, Paul E. Green attempted to define the attitudes toward risk held by each of sixteen respondents (four each from a firm's sales, production, finance, and research departments). His first significant finding was that curves expressing individuals' utility functions were not linear with respect to percent return on investment. He discovered a general disinclination to gamble with wide variability in returns, and a preference for relatively sure gambles which could lead to acceptable returns. His results were strongly indicative of general support for gambles likely to attain a 20 percent return on investment (the target figure for the company in question). As one might suspect, there was strong aversion to alternatives which appeared likely to attain less than the target figure (especially among the lower-level managers). Furthermore, and perhaps surprisingly, there was also demonstrable reluctance to undertake gambles which offered the expectation of greater than average returns. Conceivably, the higher expected returns may have led to the conclusion that the projects were more risky—e.g., a greater variability in returns was to be expected—even though there was no real evidence in support of this contention.

Thus more certain gambles were chosen over those with a higher expected value if the latter represented a combination of a much higher payoff weighted by a lower likelihood of realization. While it is difficult to make any general conclusion from Green's data, he does picture three utility functions, one each for a manager from the areas of research, sales, and finance. The marketing manager attached significantly more utility than his other two counterparts to gambles involving very high rates of return, those promising up to 35 percent. While the finance and research managers were quite close in their thinking, the finance manager was the more conservative by a small margin. Overall, however, on the basis of statistical analysis, Green concluded that functional allegiance had no apparent affect on attitudes toward risk.

From the studies conducted by Green, Grayson, and Swalm, noted above, we may conclude that any argument about whether or not the investment and financing models developed in the earlier sections of this book have any descriptive or normative significance must be tempered by the fact that businessmen can and probably do treat risk in something other than actuarial fashion. If one's functional allegiance (marketing, production, or finance) does not significantly affect one's attitude toward risk, then there will be common reactions by the various functional managers to those models cited which make attempts to deal with risky or uncertain situations. But suppose that attitudes toward risk differ among various types of business managers; from the studies cited, we have some basis for believing that this might be the case. An important source of conflict within the firm has now been identified. For in this event the same data can lead to materially different conclusions as to what action should be taken.

So little has been done in the way of objective analysis designed to measure attitudes of businessmen toward risk—and in comparing the attitudes of various types of managers in this respect—that it is hard to come to any conclusion as to how much the decisions of the various functional managers should be adjusted to take account of differences in the perception of risk. In absence of conclusive research or relevant experience, it is dangerous to rely on stereotypes. For example, one might look on the marketing manager in terms of the "wheeler-dealer" profile, i.e., one willing to throw caution to the winds if the pot at the end of the rainbow is sufficiently large. Similarly, the production manager with a background in engineering might be looked on as being more conservative. Even though Green's samples and methodology do not lead to any firm conclusions, apparently he did not find significant differences in attitudes toward risk among the four classes of managers studied. However, Swalm's study showed definite differences in attitudes towards risk among managers. To what extent these contrary conclusions stem from differences in methodology is not really clear.

At this point perhaps a summary of the argument will be appreciated. A firm's financial decisions are typically made in a world of uncertainty. The search for a defensible basis on which to make such decisions leads necessarily into attempts to define and specify subjective outcomes and to estimate the likelihood of their occurrence. But even after this is done, in making a decision one must always take account of his willingness to face situations which involve varying degrees of risk—or more properly estimated uncertainty. This logically can be a source of differing opinions among managers in the functional areas as to what alternatives a firm should pursue, and conflicts of this type ultimately are resolved one way or another.

Who does this and on what basis is not our concern here. We merely wish to make sure that the nature of the conflict is understood. By way of pinpointing another problem before passing on to other issues, let us suggest the additional and interesting possibility that one's ability to fix outcomes and estimate likelihoods of occurrence might be to some extent a function of his attitudes toward risk. Assume, for example, a manager who is strongly adverse to the assumption of risk. For him the utility of successively more profitable but increasingly more risky alternatives would not be proportional to increases in their expected value measured in monetary terms. Asking such a person to estimate outcomes and associated likelihood of occurrence conceivably could lead to biased measures. For example, he might tend to underestimate the value attached to outcomes with a low chance of being realized, or to understate their likelihoods of occurrence. In effect, he would generate data that would tend to reinforce his own willingness to accept increasingly risky but potentially lucrative ventures, and conceivably this could be done unconsciously.

In any analysis of the firm's decision-making processes, one must admit the possibility that such bias occurs. Even though the staff personnel that generate data may consciously seek to do their job in an objective fashion, unconsciously they can be influenced by their knowledge of how the line managers to whom they report feel about risk and uncertainty. In decision-making models which involve the subjective conversion of uncertainty to risk, it is to management and not to staff personnel that the firm ultimately turns for the estimation of the likelihood of various alternatives.

In this respect it can be charged that discussions of management decision making emphasize model building at the expense of greater consideration being given to problems with the data on which they are based. Perhaps this helps explain the difficulty some students have in appreciating why decision making is in practice such a sticky problem, when some of the models and related theories are so simple. While the focus of this book is on the finance manager and the decisions he must make, it is also greatly concerned with the data which support his decisions. For a given decision-making model, changes in data can clearly result in changes in recommended courses of action.

Differences in Perception of Firm Goals

Another influence on executive decisions is differences in perception of the goals of the firm. In discussing this issue we give only passing mention to the previous debate over whether firms can have goals at all. Clearly the large firm with multiple levels of decision making cannot be directed to identifiable ends as readily as can the one-man enterprise. The collective result of all the attempts to shape the firm's development may lead ultimately in directions which are undefinable through any conventional type of analysis. Then there is some support for the view that a large business firm is in reality a system which runs itself, and which in effect shapes its managers' behavior, rather than the opposite. Ignoring the sophistication of the issue for the moment, let us assume that businessmen generally act as if they have some idea of their firm's goals and some faith in their ability to direct its activities to definite ends.

It is difficult to find empirical support for the views that the functional managers possess any common perception of firm goals. Nor is there any evidence available to conclusively document the extent to which lack of agreement on goals is a real problem in functional coordination. Yet this is a source of difficulty. As evidence we cite the volumes that have been written on the importance of and techniques for setting corporate objectives, and the adverse consequences of not having objectives, or having ones that are vague, ambiguous, or not otherwise clearly defined. Commonly shared perceptions of firm objectives supply the functional managers with a type of corporate utility function, an alter ego, which helps give a consistency to their actions, even though these may be taken independently and in absence of consultation.

The functional manager attains his status by virtue of his ability to establish, interpret, and accomplish corporate objectives, and in the process it may be argued that he develops a corporate "personality" which is quite distinct from his personality as an individual. But just as there are differences in managers' individual personalities which affect how they react and the types of decisions they make as individuals, there are also differences in managers' corporate personalities, which affect how they react and the types of decisions they make as managers.

The problem of differences in goal perception is compounded by the fact that while wealth maximization as postulated previously does lend itself to precise definition, it may not be operationally useful for all firms, since it is a long-run concept and as such might be mitigated by short-run strategies. All other things being equal, there may be far less disagreement over how to maximize the firm's profits over the coming year than how to maximize wealth over the next twenty years.

A second source of problems stems from the necessity that functional managers face of restating overall corporate objectives in terms of operational standards. The successive redefinition and fragmentation of overall goals that occurs as one goes down the organizational hierarchy is needed if the total pattern of activity ultimately is to bear some relationship to the firm's overall goals or objectives. But even if the functional manager feeds in an accurate perception of the latter at the top, there is no guarantee that this perception will not become changed or distorted along the way. The goal of corporate wealth maximization as it moves closer and closer to individuals with less corporate experience, less managerial and corporate identification, is more and more likely to suggest courses of action that conflict with alternatives leading in the direction of individual rather than corporate wealth maximization. Thus the manager cannot assume that a common corporate personality will serve to coordinate efforts at lower levels in the firm, even though this may be the case for the top-level decision-making group. This being the case, rather elaborate control systems have been developed to synchronize corporate activities at all levels within the organization.

Differences in Visibility and Accountability

A third factor affecting the types of decisions the functional managers make is differences in their visibility and accountability. In this sense the production manager probably enjoys maximum visibility and accountability. Costs in his area are usually definable, and it is readily apparent when the production process breaks down, given the detailed records available concerning his output, coupled with the fact that customers or the other two functional managers readily make production failures known to top management. In all cases the production manager's failure affects their ability to carry out their goals.

While the marketing manager is highly visible, it may be argued that implicitly he is held less accountable than the other two functional managers. He can be looked on as being in an inherently poorer position to directly influence performance than are the other two, inasmuch as far fewer factors are under his direct control. Furthermore, by the nature of his job he inherits a far greater responsibility for adapting to his environment. Demand for a firm's products is not only a function of such controllable factors as price and promotion but is also affected by often relatively difficult-to-change commitments to product and channel of distribution, and by actions of competitors, government, and consumers over which the marketing manager may have little or no influence. For these and other reasons it emerges as a supportable conclusion that the marketing manager, personalities ignored, is held less accountable for failure to reach planned objectives than is typically the case with his functional counterparts.

It is difficult to position the finance manager as to his visibility and accountability. It can be argued that if his plans fall short of attainment to the point that liquidity problems develop, this will automatically precipitate a corporate crisis. Thus, even though his plans and decisions may assume as an input that the other managers will accomplish certain minimum objectives, it appears that there is less tolerance toward failures in the financial area than in the other two. After all, one of the finance manager's tasks is to anticipate the possibility of subpar performance in other areas through, for example, the maintenance of adequate reserves. Furthermore, a liquidity problem represents an immediate threat to corporate existence, while lower-than-average sales or higher-than-average production costs may be looked on as merely the manifestation of the problem and not the problem per se.

It is with respect to the long-run problems of wealth maximization that the finance manager is far less visible and accountable. To begin with, it is clearly recognized that the firm's long-run objectives are accomplished in a world of uncertainty, and hindsight permits many reasonable explanations of why things didn't work out precisely as anticipated. If satisfactory rather than maximum contributions to wealth are an acceptable standard of performance, then this may be sufficient if the firm maintains its relative position in the economy and its industry. Thus a satisfactory contribution to wealth may not necessarily be examined from the standpoint that others might have been more satisfactory, or might conceivably have led to *maximization* of wealth.

Finally, with respect to the financial manager, if he can avoid liquidity problems in the short run, it may take quite some time to determine how effective he is in accomplishing the firm's longer-run goals. For this and the reasons cited above, a reasonable conclusion is that the finance manager, if he can avoid liquidity problems, is less visible and accountable than his two top-level counterparts. And if the three functional managers differ in this important respect, their attitudes toward any given problem and the types of decisions they make can be affected.

Differences in Incentives

Inasmuch as executives typically receive from 30 to 50 percent of their compensation from incentive plans, the influence of such plans on executive decisions cannot be ignored. In discussing differences in incentives, we refer not to the incentives managers receive as individuals but the formal incentives they receive as managers. In this respect, what we are concerned with here are those incentive systems which treat managers in the functional areas differently. In recent years there has been a tendency toward the elimination of such plans in favor of looking on top management as a group. While the relative extent of their participation in incentive schemes may differ, at least the amount of incentive compensation received is calculated with reference to some common base statistic.

One significant difference in this respect is a greater than average tendency for marketing managers' compensation to be related to some direct measure of performance in their functional area. Logically this is an outgrowth of the established practice of paying salesmen's commissions, and the fact that ex-salesmen frequently move up into sales-management positions. If the star salesman doesn't always become the sales manager, at least a generally satisfactory sales record is required. Thus if the individual was successfully motivated by incentive compensation at the field-sales level, it was a logical transition to perpetuate incentive compensation at the managerial level.

It might be noted that the recent development of the managerial approach to marketing has probably served to counter the trend toward incentive payment in the marketing area noted above. In fact, it can be argued that incentives based on volume can make it difficult to take a customer-oriented approach, and if incentives are to be offered in this area at all they should be based on other factors such as profits, growth in sales, growth in new sales, etc. Presumably, the justification for exploring other bases for incentive payment is to avoid as much as possible tendencies toward suboptimization.

Historically, one also finds precedent for offering production managers incentives based on some measure of performance in their department. Not only have recent years seen production managers being taken in under the top-management umbrella, but their incentive schemes have also been modified. One reaction to the tendencies toward suboptimization which developed under relatively simple schemes, which were a direct function of output, was to make them considerably more complex, taking into account a great number of factors. But as the complexity of such schemes increased beyond a certain point, their ability to influence behavior started to decline. In designing incentive schemes, one faces the real dilemma that control of tendencies to suboptimization may be at the expense of their ability to motivate.

In conclusion, there is no clear-cut evidence to support the contention that functional managers today are led to think differently because of differences in incentive schemes which are in turn the source of significant differences in their compensation. This does not mean that managers in the three principal functional areas are necessarily compensated equally, although data relating to the latter point are difficult to find.

Differences in Frame of Reference

For lack of a better way of putting it, let us consider briefly how the ability of the functional executives to arrive at decisions may be affected by differences in their frames of reference. Under this heading we include several miscellaneous factors which are difficult to categorize separately. The production manager's job often differs from the other two functional jobs in that a high proportion of those who work within his department are unionized employees. Thus he must consider the effect of almost any decision on the firm's labor relations. Also, the production manager frequently is responsible for more employees than either of the other managers, although in a sales-oriented or service-oriented operation this need not be the case.

The marketing manager, by way of comparison, tends to operate within the framework of a white-collar world. For him, experience with labor unions or minority groups is far less likely. On the other hand, he usually has first-hand experience with that type of employee frequently looked on as constituting a special case: the salesman. In the event that the firm has an outside sales force, he will be aware of the many problems encountered in trying to direct and stimulate the efforts of employees over which he may have little direct control. If advertising is a key factor in stimulating demand for the firm's products, he will be experienced in dealing with a specialized service supplied the firm by outsiders who are paid usually in direct proportion to how much the firm spends (commonly 15 percent of media costs). Or, if advertising is handled internally, the marketing manager must deal with the much-debated problem of how to harness creativity and direct it to definite corporate objectives.

There are also experiences which are largely unique to finance managers, and which cannot but serve to color their outlook to business decisions. The nature of their job leads to thinking in financial terms, and frequently their contacts with financial intermediaries external to the firm will throw them into association with others who think in similar terms. Further, there is always the possibility that relations may be strained between the finance and the accounting manager, especially if the latter looks on himself as having advisory responsibilities which extend very far beyond the mere provision of routine financial data. Thus a finance manager who feels his position in the power structure is threatened by the accounting manager may act differently in given situations from one who does not feel that this is the case.

The nature of the firm, the competitive structure of its industry, the relative importance of production and marketing, the pace of technology, and trends in demand for its products—these are only a few of the many diverse factors that can serve to differentiate the frames of reference within which the functional managers operate.

Individual Differences

Finally, let us make brief mention of a very obvious source of differences of opinion among managers—those that stem from the fact that their personalities differ. Popular literature on management tends to leave students with the idea that advancement to the top of the corporate hierarchy involves acceptance of conformity to the extent that by then individual personality differences, for all practical purposes, have disappeared. Attending only a single top-level committee meeting or board of directors meeting hardly reinforces such a conclusion. Clearly there is no single "manager" profile—

or even a limited number of identifiable such profiles. Individual differences do exist, and it is difficult to imagine how a firm could compete in the contemporary business climate if it did not attempt to capitalize on such differences.

The Systemic Approach

The systemic approach can be quite useful in describing what occurs in a complex organization such as a business firm, and in analyses to determine the interactions and interdependencies of the management functions. The authors view the finance function in management as being the common denominator and the analytical basis for evaluating the efficiency with which the companion functions of management, production, and marketing are carried out in an organization or system.

As was pointed out in Chapter 1, the *process* or *adaptive system* model is perhaps most relevant to business organizations since it suggests activity and change through time rather than static immobility. In accepting the systemic view of the firm, and stressing the quantifiable, the analysis of organizational efficiency may be placed under the rubric, "systems analysis." The whole of the organization process is subject to analyses in terms of costs and benefits to optimize productive efficiency for the total system and thereby optimize wealth accumulation.

SUMMARY AND CONCLUSIONS

Investment and financing decisions are improperly termed financial-management decisions. They commit the firm's resources to definite ends and can be looked on only as top management decisions which are properly the concern of the entire management group. Or, to put it another way, increasingly we find that all managers are being trained to think in financial terms, even though their functional allegiance may be to other areas of the firm's activity. For most firms the day is long since gone when each of the functional managers was narrowly trained in and operated only within the bounds of his own area of functional specialization. In the education of managers and would-be managers, one finds trends toward integration of subject matter formerly taught in separate courses and offered by functionally-identified departments or instructors. Indeed, this book represents one attempt to move in that direction, i.e., to utilize the systemic approach. Another education reflection of this reality of the business world is the Master of Business Administration degree, with its insistence on broad preparation to encompass all the functional areas, and the current managerial emphasis being given to undergraduate studies in business.

Even though there is a developing trend for a firm's top-management group to be better informed in the techniques of financial management, there is still no universal agreement as to how the largely normative concepts set forth in the preceding chapters should be applied. Furthermore, in order to get a "solution" in most cases one must have satisfactorily coped with the problem of reducing uncertainty to some sort of a risk equivalent. Subjective probabilities represent nothing more than an attempt to adapt precise experience in a form which will support objective analysis. Thus, even though the executive group may start with a common acceptance and understanding of the firm's goals, and may be of a like mind as to the decision model which will be applied, there still remains the very real problem of giving values, in terms of utility preferences, to the inputs when one is planning ahead over some future period in time.

This chapter highlights only a few of the problems which the organization must deal with if it is to clearly understand the bases on which its resource allocation decisions are made. While many of the features of the situations studied are amenable to computerized statement, and although the system itself can be machine-simulated, if human behavior affects the inputs it is clear that someone cognizant of that behavior—its forms and consequences—must be the final judge of the output.

SUGGESTED REFERENCES

Alderson, Wroe, and Paul F. Green, *Planning and Problem Solving in Marketing*. Homewood, Ill.: Richard D. Irwin, Inc., 1964, pp. 162–166.

Batten, J. D., "Orienting A New Marketing Manager: An Uncommon Approach," *Business Management*, 32 (June 1967), pp. 101–102.

Boulding, Kenneth E., "Implications for General Economics of More Realistic Theories of the Firm," *American Economic Review*, 32 (May 1952), pp. 35–44.

Green, Paul E., "Risk Attitudes and Chemical Investment Decisions," *Chemical Engineering Progress* (January 1963), p. 35.

Hindricks, H. J., "Finance on the Frontier," *Financial Executive*, 32 (March 1964), pp. 51–54.

Kilpatrick, Franklin P. (ed.), *Explorations in Transactional Psychology*. New York: New York University Press, 1961.

March, James G., and Herbert A. Simon, *Organizations*. New York: John Wiley & Sons, Inc., 1958.

McGann, T. J., "Controller Belongs on Marketing Team," *Controller*, 29 (August 1961), pp. 377–382.

Swalm, Ralph O., "Utility Theory . . . Insights into Risk Taking," *Harvard Business Review*, 44 (November–December 1966), pp. 123–138.

Supplementary References

BOOKS

Bogen, Jules I. (ed.), *Financial Handbook*. New York: The Ronald Press Company, 1964.

Brech, E., and L. Urwick, *The Making of Scientific Management: Thirteen Pioneers*, Vol. I. London: Management Publications Trust, 1949.

Buffa, Elwood, *Modern Production Management*. New York: John Wiley & Sons, Inc., 1965.

Cox, Reavis, Charles S. Goodman, and Thomas C. Fichandler, *Distribution in a High Level Economy*. Englewood Cliffs, N.J.: Prentice-Hall, Inc., 1965.

Dewing, Arthur S., *The Financial Policy of Corporations*. New York: Ronald Press Company, 1920.

Garrett, Leonard J., and Milton Silver, *Production Management Analysis*. New York: Harcourt, Brace & World, Inc., 1965.

Guthman, Harry G., and Herbert E. Dougall, *Corporate Financial Policy*. Englewood Cliffs, N.J.: Prentice-Hall, Inc., 1962.

Howard, John A., *Marketing Management: Analysis and Planning*. Rev. ed. Homewood, Ill.: Richard D. Irwin, Inc., 1963.

Levy, Lester S., and Roy J. Sampson, *American Economic Development: Growth of the U.S. in the Western World*. Boston: Allyn and Bacon, Inc,. 1962.

Lindsay, Robert, and Arnold Sametz, *Financial Management—An Analytical Approach*. Homewood, Ill.: Richard D. Irwin, Inc., 1964.

Revzan, David A., *Wholesaling in Marketing Organization*. New York: John Wiley & Sons, Inc., 1961.

Robichek, Alexander A., and Stewart C. Myers, *Optimal Financing Decisions*. Englewood Cliffs, N.J.: Prentice-Hall, Inc., 1965.

Solomon, Ezra, *The Theory of Financial Management*. New York: Columbia University Press, 1963.

Starr, Martin K., *Production Management: Systems and Synthesis.* Engle-
wood Cliffs, N.J.: Prentice-Hall, Inc., 1964.
Weston, J. Fred, *Managerial Finance.* Holt, Rinehart and Winston, Inc., 1962
———, *The Scope and Methodology of Finance.* Englewood Cliffs, N.J.:
Prentice-Hall, Inc., 1966.

STUDIES

National Industrial Conference Board, "The Duties of Financial Executives,"
Studies in Business Policy (No. 56, 1952), pp. 17–19.
American Management Association, "The Financial Executives' Job," *Finan-
cial Management Series* (No. 99, 1952), pp. 3–37.

ARTICLES

Bosland, Chelcie C., Francis J. Calkins, Donald M. Halley, Pearson Hunt,
Miller Upton, "Materials and Methods of Teaching Business Finance,"
Journal of Finance, 5 (September 1950), pp. 270–292.
Dauten, Carl A., "The Necessary Ingredients of a Theory of Business Fi-
nance," *Journal of Finance,* 10 (May 1955), pp. 107–120.
Plummer, George, and George Moller, "The Financial Executive," *The Con-
troller,* 30 (January 1962), pp. 16–32.
Robbins, Sidney, and Edward Foster, "Profit Planning and the Finance Func-
tion," *Journal of Finance,* 12 (December 1957), pp. 451–467.
Solomon, Ezra, "What Should We Teach in a Course in Business Finance,"
Journal of Finance, 21 (May 1966), pp. 411–415.
Weston, J. Fred, "The Finance Function," *Journal of Finance,* 9 (September
1954), pp. 265–282.
———, "Toward Theories of Financial Policies," *Journal of Finance,* 10
(May 1955), pp. 130–143.